Chinese

Learn Mandarin Chinese for Beginners: A Simple Guide That Will Help You on Your Language Learning Journey

© **Copyright 2019**

All Rights Reserved. No part of this book may be reproduced in any form without permission in writing from the author. Reviewers may quote brief passages in reviews.

Disclaimer: No part of this publication may be reproduced or transmitted in any form or by any means, mechanical or electronic, including photocopying or recording, or by any information storage and retrieval system, or transmitted by email without permission in writing from the publisher.

While all attempts have been made to verify the information provided in this publication, neither the author nor the publisher assumes any responsibility for errors, omissions or contrary interpretations of the subject matter herein.

This book is for entertainment purposes only. The views expressed are those of the author alone, and should not be taken as expert instruction or commands. The reader is responsible for his or her own actions.

Adherence to all applicable laws and regulations, including international, federal, state and local laws governing professional licensing, business practices, advertising and all other aspects of doing business in the US, Canada, UK or any other jurisdiction is the sole responsibility of the purchaser or reader.

Neither the author nor the publisher assumes any responsibility or liability whatsoever on the behalf of the purchaser or reader of these materials. Any perceived slight of any individual or organization is purely unintentional.

Contents

INTRODUCTION 1
CHAPTER 1: LEARNING CHINESE TONES 3
CHAPTER 2: LEARNING BASIC CHINESE GRAMMAR 16
CHAPTER 3: HOW TO COUNT 65
CHAPTER 4: HOW TO BE POLITE WHEN SPEAKING CHINESE? 69
CHAPTER 5: GREETING AND INTRODUCTION 80
CHAPTER 6: DAILY LIFE AND SOCIAL ACTIVITY 94
CONCLUSION 103

Introduction

Welcome to *Chinese: Learn Mandarin Chinese for Beginners: A Simple Guide That Will Help You on Your Language Learning Journey*! This will be your first step toward success during the process of Chinese study.

There are only 10 chapters in this book. However, after learning these chapters, a solid foundation will be established both in pronunciation and basic knowledge of the Chinese language. In addition, you will also master some words and expressions for daily communication.

If you want to impress a future audience with your "perfect" spoken Chinese, a lot of time and effort while studying this book will need to be invested. Not only will you need to master the 3 basic elements of pronunciation (i.e. initials, vowels, and most importantly, tones), but you will also have to understand the sound change in certain circumstances.

Perhaps you may have heard people complaining that Chinese is difficult to learn. However, after studying this book, you will find that it is indeed not true. After finishing this book, you will easily master some Chinese expressions. A solid foundation is thus laid for advanced study in the future.

In addition to Chinese pronunciation, this book will also familiarize you with dialogue commonly used in daily communication.

Examples include greeting, how to introduce yourself and other people, educational background, work, family, and friends, likes and dislikes, food and drink, and other common topics. You will have a sense of accomplishment after finishing these 10 chapters, because you will be able to speak quite a few idiomatic sentences which will enable you to have basic communications with native speakers. If you find that some translations in this book feel unnatural in English, we want you to note that we've used the literal method on purpose so that differences between the language systems can be stressed.

Chinese: Learn Mandarin Chinese for Beginners: A Simple Guide That Will Help You on Your Language Learning Journey is the key to entering the world of the Chinese language. We hope you find it fun and wish you success!

Chapter 1: Learning Chinese Tones

Among the components of a Chinese syllable, there is a tone besides the initial and the final. Generally speaking, one Chinese character corresponds to one syllable. A Chinese syllable can have no initials, but must have a final and a tone. Syllables with the same initials and finals but in different tones usually have different meanings.

Chinese has four main tones, as follows:

The main vocal characteristic of the first tone is high and flat. When it is articulated, the vocal cords are tightened up and the pitch is kept at a relatively higher level for a while. Let's see some examples so you can understand it better:

参加, cān jiā, to take part in/to join

今天, jīn tiān, today

沙发, shā fā, sofa

香蕉, xiāng jiāo, banana

司机, sī jī, driver

分钟, fēn zhōng, minute

应该, yīng gāi, should

西餐, xī cān, western food.

关系, guān xì, relationship/in relation to

春天, chūn tiān, spring

抒发, shū fā, to express

通知, tōng zhī, notice/to inform

The second tone is a rising tone. It rises from the middle to a higher level while the vocal cords are gradually tightened up. Let's see some examples so you can understand it better:

回答, huí dá, to answer

集合, jí hé, assemblage/to gather

明年, míng nián, next year.

篮球, lán qiú, basketball

年级, nián jí, grade

同学, tóng xué, classmate

厨房, chúfáng, kitchen

从前, cóng qián, in the past

留学, liú xué, to study abroad

邮局, yóu jú, post office

原来, yuán lái, turn out to be

儿童, ér tóng, small child

The third tone is a dipping tone. The pitch goes from middle to low, then to high. Let's see some examples so you can understand it better:

辅导, fǔ dǎo, to coach

可以, kě yǐ, should/sure

了解, liǎo jiě, to understand

手表, shǒu biǎo, watch

所以. suǒ yǐ, therefore/so

洗澡, xǐ zǎo, take a shower

小姐, xiǎo jiě, Ms.

语法, yǔ fǎ, grammar

也许, yě xǔ, maybe/perhaps

只好, zhǐ hǎo, have to

When the fourth tone is pronounced, the vocal cords are first tightened and then relaxed. The voice hence rapidly falls from the higher to the lower level. It is relatively easy to pronounce for most people. Let's see some examples so you can understand it better:

毕业, bì yè, to graduate

宿舍, sù shè, dormitory

大概, dà gài, probably

锻炼, duàn liàn, to exercise

运动, yùn dòng, sport

介绍, jiè shào, to introduce

画报, huà bào, pictorial

教授, jiào shòu, professor

庆祝, qìng zhù, to celebrate

继续, jì xù, continue

饭店, fàn diàn, restaurant

过去, guò qù, in the past/to come over

Intensive Practice

Now, let's practice with more vocabulary mixed by different tones.

1. First tone and second tone.

当然, dāng rán, of course

科学, kē xué, science

非常, fēi cháng, extremely/very

刚才, gāng cái, just now/a moment ago

欢迎, huān yíng, welcome

生词, shēng cí, new vocabulary

中文, zhōng wén, Chinese

私人, sī rén, personal/ private

家庭, jiā tíng, home

青年, qīng nián, youth

将来, jiāng lái, future

要求, yāo qiú, requirement/to ask

房间, fáng jiān, room

国家, guó jiā, country

离开, lí kāi, to leave

明天, míng tiān, tomorrow

同屋, tóng wū, roommate

毛衣, máo yī, sweater

结婚, jié hūn, to get married

时间, shí jiān, time

邻居, lín jū, neighbor

昨天, zuó tiān, yesterday

提高, tí gāo, to improve

毛巾, máo jīn, towel

2. First tone and third tone.

方法, fāng fǎ, method

身体, shēn tǐ, body

听写, tīng xiě, dictation

英语, yīng yǔ, English

班长, bān zhǎng, monitor

东北, dōng běi, northeast

黑板, hēi bǎn, blackboard

风景, fēng jǐng, landscape

宾馆, bīn guǎn, hotel

中午, zhōng wǔ, noon

出版, chū bǎn, to publish

开始, kāi shǐ, to start

火车, huǒ chē, train

好吃, hǎo chī, delicious

紧张, jǐn zhāng, nervous

简单, jiǎn dān, simple

老师, lǎo shī, teacher

母亲, mǔ qīn, mother

首都, shǒu dū, capital

许多, xǔ duō, many

已经, yǐ jīng, already

语音, yǔ yīn, voice

3. First tone and fourth tone.

帮助, bāng zhù, to help,

车站, chē zhàn, station,

方便, fāng biàn, convenient

高兴, gāo xìng, happy

鸡蛋, jī dàn, egg

天气, tiān qì, weather

温度, wēn dù, temperature

相信, xiāng xìn, to believe

因为, yīn wéi, because

通过, tōng guò, to pass

干净, gàn jìng, clean

丰富, fēng fù, colorful

汽车, qì chē, automobile

教师, jiào shī, teacher

上班, shàng bān, to go to work

大约, dà yuē, roughly/probably

电梯, diàn tī, elevator/ lifter

放心, fàng xīn, to relax

健康, jiàn kāng, health

日期, rì qī, date

外教, wài jiào, foreign teacher

后天, hòu tiān, the day after tomorrow

对方, duì fāng, the other side

进修, jìn xiū, to get trained

4. Second tone and third tone.

词典, cí diǎn, dictionary

而且, ér qiě, and

牛奶, niú nǎi, milk

没有, méi yǒu, no

门口, mén kǒu, doorway

苹果, píng guǒ, apple

球场, qiú chǎng, field

游泳, yóu yǒng, swimming

人口, rén kǒu, population

从此, cóng cǐ, from then on

传统, chuán tǒng, tradition

厘米, lí mǐ, centimeter

解决, jiě jué, to solve

旅行, lǚ xíng, to travel

起床, qǐ chuáng, to get up

请求, qǐng qiú, to ask/requirement

水平, shuǐ píng, level

小时, xiǎo shí, hour

选择, xuǎn zé, to choose/choice

以为, yǐ wéi, to think

语言, yǔ yán, language

主人, zhǔ rén, master/host

5. Second tone and fourth tone.

不错, bú cuò, not bad

迟到, chí dào, late

合适, hé shì, suitable

劳驾, láo jià, excuse me

邮票, yóu piào, stamp

服务, fú wù, service/to serve

年纪, nián jì, age

皮带, pí dài, belt

然后, rán hòu, then

节日, jié rì, festival

成绩, chéng jì, grade

伯父, bó fù, uncle

不行, bùxíng, no way

联系, lián xì, to contact

认为, rèn wéi, to think

上学, shàng xué, to go to school

太阳, tài yáng, sun

预习, yù xí, to preview

季节, jìjié, season

电池, diàn chí, battery

绿茶, lǜ chá, green tea

气球, qì qiú, balloon

后年, hòu nián, the year after next year

外国, wài guó, foreign country

6. Third tone and fourth tone.

比较, bǐ jiào, to compare

感谢, gǎn xiè, to thank

好看, hǎo kàn, good looking

考试, kǎo shì, exam

礼物, lǐ wù, gift

满意, mǎn yì, satisfying

米饭, mǐ fàn, rice

讨论, tǎo lùn, to discuss

晚会, wǎn huì, banquet

早饭, zǎo fàn, breakfast

办法, bàn fǎ, method

剧场, jù chǎng, theater

记者, jì zhě, journalist

大小, dà xiǎo, size

刻苦, kè kǔ, hardworking

要紧, yào jǐn, important

政府, zhèng fǔ, government

课本, kè běn, textbook

道理, dào lǐ, principle

电子, diàn zǐ, electron / electronic

不久, bú jiǔ, soon after/ shortly

号码, hào mǎ, number

It's highly recommended to hear the tones demonstrated by a native speaker since it's hard to get an idea of what they sound like purely through text.

Additional Knowledge

Generally speaking, the tone of each syllable in Chinese is fixed. However, when two or more than two syllables are pronounced together, there is sometimes a tonal modulation which is called "Tone Sandhi". Here are some tips for you to pronounce much more accurately in accordance with Tone Sandhi. These might be too hard for beginners, so just read and try if you are interested.

1. When two adjacent syllables both carry third tones, the first syllable must be pronounced as the second tone. For example: 你好 (nǐ hǎo) must be pronounced as ní hǎo and 可以 (kě yǐ) must be pronounced as ké yǐ.

2. When a third tone syllable is followed by syllables of the other three tones, and most syllables are with a neutral tone, only the first half of the third tone is pronounced.

3. Some syllables in Chinese are pronounced both short and lightly. This is called the neutral tone. The neutral tone always appears after another syllable or between other syllables. It cannot appear as the first syllable of a word or a sentence. In a disyllabic word with reduplicated syllables, the second syllable is usually read in the neutral tone. Apart from that, there is no simple or easy way to learn neutral tones. They must be learned, memorized, and mastered one by one.

4. The pitch of a neutral tone varies according to the tone of the syllable that comes before it. Normally, when it comes after a first, second, or fourth tone, its pitch is relatively low. Only when it comes after a third tone does its pitch become relatively higher.

5. There is a retroflex final "er" in the finals of Chinese. It is not used to combine with other initials, but forms a syllable on its own. For example, 儿(ér) is often used as a suffix. After a long time of liaison, its pronunciation is transformed in such a way that it is pronounced together with the syllable that comes before it as a single unit. This phenomenon is called retro-flexion.

6. When it is read independently or is at the end of a word, 一is pronounced as yī; when it precedes a 1st, 2nd, or a 3rd tone, 一is pronounced as yì ; when it precedes a 4th tone, 一is pronounced as yí.

7. The tone of 不 does not change when it stands by itself or precedes a 1st, 2nd or a 3rd tone, pronounced as bù, but it is pronounced as bú when it precedes a 4th tone.

If you can master these, you will become an excellent Chinese speaker.

Warm up

Memorizing vocabulary is important to every learner, but accuracy is even more important. When you learn a character, you're expected to pronounce it correctly by using the right tone because different pronunciations could have entirely different meanings.

Once you have a basic grasp of vocabulary and pronunciation, you can move on to basic conversational phrases which are used in everyday Chinese speech. Starting with practicing basic conversational Chinese will allow you to get familiar with the language. Now let's practice; we will analyze the phrases afterwards.

你好 （nǐ hǎo）。Hello/How are you?

早上好 （zǎo shang hǎo）。Good morning.

下午好 （xià wǔ hǎo）。Good afternoon.

晚上好 （wǎn shang hǎo）。Good evening.

晚安 （wǎn ān）。Good night.

你叫什么名字 （nǐ jiào shén me míng zì）？What is your name?

是的 （shì de）。Yes.

不是 （bú shì）。No.

谢谢你 （xiè xie nǐ）。Thank you.

不用谢 （bú yòng xiè）。You're welcome./My pleasure.

对不起 （duì bù qǐ）。Excuse me/sorry.

我不懂（wǒ bù dǒng）。I don't understand.

再见（zài jiàn）。Goodbye.

没关系（méi guān xi）。It's okay.

明天见（míng tiān jiàn）。See you tomorrow.

请进（qǐng jìn）。Come in please.

认识你很高兴（rèn shi nǐ hěn gāo xìng）。It's nice to meet you.

How do you feel so far? Do you have a feeling that you have already mastered a little bit Chinese? Well, if you can speak the above sentences fluently with correct tones, your Chinese listeners will besurprised.

Chapter 2: Learning Basic Chinese Grammar

It's easy to get a headache and be bored when talking about grammar. Chinese grammar is especially hard even for native speakers. But in this book, no attempt has been made to give a comprehensive or systematic account of Chinese grammar; only essential points will be introduced. So don't dread this part too much. Learning some basic grammar is really helpful for you to further your study in the Chinese language.

To ease the task for our dear learner, brief notes have been given for the more difficult expressions in the texts to facilitate your understanding of the Chinese language. The classification of Chinese sentence patterns is a rather complicated question. The patterns listed in this book are solely for reference.

Nouns, adjectives, pronouns

Nouns are words that denote people or things. Those nouns that are the names of people, places, and organizations are called proper nouns. In Chinese sentences, nouns normally function as subjects, objects, or attributes. We will analyze some special classes of nouns later.

Adjectives are the words that describe the shape, quality, or state of a person or a thing. In Chinese sentences, adjectives normally function as predicates, attributes, adverbials, or complements.

Nouns and adjectives are very easy. What you need to do is when you hear a word in English, think about how you would say it in Chinese. If you don't know how to say it, write it down and look it up later. It's handy to keep a little notebook with you for this purpose. Attach little Chinese labels (with the character, the pinyin and the pronunciation) to items around your house, such as the mirror, the TV, and chairs. You'll see the words so often that you'll learn them without realizing it.

Pronouns are the words that stand for nouns, verbs, and adjectives. Chinese pronouns are classified as personal pronouns, demonstrative pronouns, and interrogative pronouns. In Chinese sentences, pronouns normally function as subjects, objects, or attributes. Now, let's talk about the three different kinds of pronouns one by one.

1. Personal pronoun

你/您 (nǐ/nín), you

Both of them are second person singular pronouns. 你 (nǐ) is the usual form while 您 (nín) is the honorific or polite form. The plural of 你 (nǐ) is formed by the suffix 们 (men). The plural of 您 (nín) is formed by using a numeral. Occasionally 您们 (nín men) appears in writing, but it is never used in spoken Chinese.

我们/咱们 （wǒ men/zán men), we/us

Both of them are first person plural pronouns. However, 咱们 (zán men) includes the speaker and the person spoken to, while 我们 (wǒ men) may be inclusive or exclusive, i.e. the person spoken to may be included or excluded. Please pay attention here, 我 (wǒ) is a first person singular pronoun, but 咱 (zán) can seldom be used as a singular pronoun. Without 们（men）, 咱（zán）, in most occasions, is still a plural pronoun.

他/她/它 (tā), him (he)/ her (she)/ it

All of them pronounced as tā, 他/她（tā）are third person singular pronouns, while 它（tā）refers to things. Their plural forms are 他们/她们/它们（tā）respectively.

Note here, 们（men）is a plural suffix. When added to a singular pronoun or singular personal noun, it makes it plural. However, 们（men） is never added to noun modified by a numeral.

2. Demonstrative pronouns

这/那（zhè/ nà）

They stand for either a person or thing. 这（zhè） refers to what is nearer to the speaker, and 那（nà）to what is farther off. For example:

这是我的车，那是他的车（zhè shì wǒ de chē, nà shì tā de chē）。

This is my car, and that's his car.

一切（yí qiè）

It is often used as an attribute to modify a noun. It denotes the whole amount or quantity of the thing or things referred to by the noun. It is often used together with 都（dōu）which occurs after 一切（yí qiè）. For example:

他的一切行李都准备好了（tā de yí qiè xíng lidōu zhǔnbèi hǎo le）。

(All of) his luggage has been prepared.

家里一切都好，不用牵挂（jiā lǐyí qièdōu hǎo, bú yòng qiān guà）。

Everything is fine at home; don't worry.

另外（lìng wài）

It is often used as an attribute to modify a noun or a quantity word. It indicates that the thing or quantity referred to is outside the range of what has been previously mentioned. Often 的（de）occurs between 另外（lìng wài）and the noun or quantity word it modifies. For example:

今天一部分时间工作，另外的时间玩电脑游戏（jīn tiān yí bù fèn shí jiān gōng zuò, lìng wài de shí jiān wán diàn nǎo yóu xì）。

Part of today's time will be used for work; the other part will be used for computer games.

一些人喜欢你，另外一些人不喜欢你（yìxiē rén xǐ huān nǐ, lìng wài yìxiē rén bù xǐ huān nǐ）。

Some people like you but others don't.

3. Interrogative pronouns

什么（shén me）

It is used in interrogative sentences, serving as an object by itself or together with a nominal element following it. For example:

你叫什么名字（nǐ jiào shén me míng zì）？

What is your name?

这是什么（zhè shì shén me）？

What's this?

谁（shuí）

The interrogative pronoun 谁（shuí）is used to ask about the name or identity of a person. For example:

他是谁（tā shì shuí）?

Who is he?

谁是王先生（shuí shì wáng xiān shēng）?

Who is Mr. Wang?

哪（nǎ）

When the interrogative pronoun 哪（nǎ） is used in a question, the structure is 哪（nǎ）+ measure word/noun + noun. For example,

哪本书（nǎ běn shū）?

Which book?

哪个国家（nǎ gè guó jiā）?

Which country?

几（jǐ）

It is used to ask about a number, usually less than ten. For example:

你女儿几岁了（nǐ nǚ ér jǐ suì le）?

How old is your daughter?

你来过中国几次（nǐ lái guò zhōng guó jǐ cì）?

How many times have you been in China?

多少（duō shǎo）

It is used to ask about numbers larger than ten. The measure word following it can be omitted. 多少（duō shǎo） can also be used to inquire about prices, usually in the sentence pattern "……多少钱（duō shǎo qián）". The basic unit of 人民币（rén mín bì）/ RMB is 元（yuán）, usually replaced by 块（kuài）in spoken Chinese. For example:

你们大学有多少学生（nǐ men dà xué yǒu duō shǎo xué shēng）?

How many students are in your university?

这个杯子多少钱（zhè gè bēi zǐ duō shǎo qián）?

How much is this cup?

怎么（zěn me）

It is used before a verb to ask about the manner or an action. For example:

这个地方怎么走（zhè gè dì fāng zěn me zǒu）?

How do I get to this place?

他怎么还不来（tā zěn me hái bú lái）?

Why is he still not coming?

哪儿（nǎ ér）

It is used to ask about the location of somebody or something. For example:

你去哪儿了（nǐ qù nǎ ér le）?

Where have you been?

我的外套在哪儿（wǒ de wài tào zài nǎ ér）?

Where is my coat?

怎么样（zěn me yàng）

It is used to ask about the condition/opinion of something or someone. For example:

明天我来接你怎么样（míng tiān wǒ lái jiē nǐ zěn me yàng）?

How about I come to pick you up tomorrow?

你的中文怎么样（nǐ de zhōng wén zěn me yàng）?

How is your Chinese?

Verb, modal verb, and adverb

Verbs are the words that express the action, behavior, or change of a person or a thing. In Chinese sentences they normally function as predicates. Chinese verbs do not need to change according to the tense. Tenses are expressed by the use of particles, some adverbs, and nouns denoting time. So verbs tend to be easier for learners compared to English. Let's discuss several verbs that appear with high frequency in daily communication.

有（yǒu）

It can be used in an existential sentence to indicate a person or thing exists somewhere. For example:

桌子上有一本书（zhuō zǐ shàng yǒu yìběn shū）。

There is a book on the table.

床底下有一只猫（chuáng dǐ xià yǒu yìzhī māo）。

There is a cat under the bed.

In the negative form of a 有（yǒu）sentence, 没有（méi yǒu）is used without a numeral classifier before the object. For example:

桌子上没有书（zhuō zǐ shàng méi yǒu shū）。

There is no book on the table.

床底下没有猫（chuáng dǐ xià méi yǒu māo）。

There is no cat under the bed.

有（yǒu）is sometimes used before a quantity word to indicate that a certain number has been reached. For example:

我认识他有十年了（wǒ rèn shí tā yǒu shí nián le）。

I've known him for like ten years.

中国的历史已经有五千年了（zhōng guó de lì shǐ yǐ jīng yǒu wǔ qiān nián le）。

China's history has reached five thousand years.

要（yào）

When used alone as a predicate, it means want/would like. It takes a noun as its object. The negative form is 不要（bú yào）. For example:

你要什么（nǐ yào shénme）？

What do you want?

我要这个，还要那个（wǒ yào zhè gè, hái yào nà gè）。

I want this, and I want that.

我要一个面包（wǒ yào yígè miàn bāo）。

I want a piece of bread.

在（zài）

It means "to be, to exist, to be living," indicating where a person or thing is. It is often followed by an object expressing place or position. The negative form is 不在（búzài）. For example:

我在图书馆，不在公园（wǒ zài tú shū guǎn, bú zài gōng yuán）。

I'm inthe library, not inthe park.

The sentence pattern "noun + 在（zài）+ noun" is widely used in Chinese to express location; it is equal to English "subject + linking verb + prepositional phrase".

Like Chinese sentences with adjectives as predicates, normally no linking verb is needed between the subject and 在（zài）……. The word 是（shì）would make the sentence rather emphatic and is used only when the speaker intends to emphasize an assertion, as if to refute a contrary statement. In such cases 是（shì）is spoken with a stress, for example:

我是在图书馆，不是在公园（wǒ shì zài tú shū guǎn, bú shì zài gōng yuán）。

I'm inthe library, not in the park.

When it is followed by a word of locality and acts as the predicate of a sentence, it indicates the location of somebody or something. For example:

我的行李在房间里（wǒ de xínglǐ zài fáng jiān lǐ）。

My luggage is in the room.

我妹妹在车上（wǒ mèi mei zài chē shàng）。

My sister is in the car.

了（liǎo）

It often occurs after another verb or an adjective as a complement. It shows that an action is likely to take place or a quality or a state of things is likely to change. 了（liǎo）is usually preceded by the structural particle 得（de）. The negative form is 不了（bù liǎo）without 得（de）. For example:

这点儿工作我一个人做得了（zhè diǎn ér gōng zuò wǒ yígè rén zuòdeliǎo）。

It is possible for me to manage this bit of work.

行李太多，一个人拿不了（xínglǐ tài duō, yígè rén ná bù liǎo）。

There will be too much luggage for one man to carry.

A "verb/ adjective + 得了（liǎo）" is similar in meaning to the English pattern "It is possible/likely to do..." while the negative form "verb/ adjective + 不了 (bù liǎo)" is often used to mean "It is impossible /unlikely to do..."

请 (qǐng)

When the verb 请 (qǐng) is used before another verb, an imperative sentence is formed, indicating a polite suggestion or hope. For example:

请坐 (qǐng zuò)。

Please sit down.

请听我说 (qǐng tīng wǒ shuō)。

Please listen to me.

还 (huán)

It is placed before a noun or a pronoun. It means to return something to somebody or somewhere. For example:

明天把书还我 (míng tiān bǎ shū huán wǒ)。

Return my book to me tomorrow.

他没还我钱 (tā méi huán wǒ qián)。

He didn't pay me back.

完 (wán)

When used after another verb, it plays a complementary role, expressing the idea that the action has been finished. It is often used in conjunction with adverbs like 已经 (yǐ jīng). For example:

我已经干完工作了 (wǒ yǐ jīng gàn wán gōng zuò le)。

I've finished working.

他已经写完作业了 (tā yǐ jīng xiě wán zuò yè le)。

He has finished writing his homework.

"Verb + 完（wán）" in Chinese may be compared to English "to finish + verb + ing." For example:

他已经复习完语法了（tā yǐ jīng fù xí wán yǔ fǎ le）。

He has finished reviewing his grammar.

她已经听完录音了（tā yǐ jīng tīng wán lù yīn le）。

She has finished listening to the recording.

While "to finish" is mainly a transitive verb, 完（wán） usually does not take an object. To express the idea "finish doing something", we must say "verb + 完（wán）+ object".

There is a group of verbs in Chinese that indicate thought or emotion such as 关心/喜欢/思念（guān xīn/ xǐ huān/ sī niàn）. Their meaning is rather abstract, and their usage is not quite the same as that of verbs in general. They may be modified by adverbs of degree such as 太/很/非常（tài/ hěn/ fēi cháng）. For example:

他太关心政治了（tā tài guān xīn zhèng zhì le）。

He cares too much about politics.

我很喜欢你（wǒ hěn xǐ huān nǐ）。

I'm very fond of you.

她非常思念你（tā fēi cháng sī niàn nǐ）。

She missed you so much.

Modal verbs express a desire, necessity, or possibility. They are often used together with verbs or adjectives to serve as predicates of sentences. When used alone, they act as other verbs. Let's learn some verbs and modal verbs those often appear in the sentences.

要（yào）

As a modal verb, it precedes a verb, indicating the wish and will to do something. For example:

我要买一辆自行车（wǒ yào mǎi yī liàng zì xíngchē）。

I'm going to buy a bike.

她要学游泳（tā yào xué yóu yǒng）。

She's going to learn swimming.

想（xiǎng）

It is usually used before a verb to express a hope or plan. For example:

我想买本书（wǒ xiǎng mǎi běn shū）。

I want to buy a book.

他想去爬山（tā xiǎng qù pá shān）。

He wants to go mountain climbing.

能（néng）

It is usually used before a verb to form the predicate indicating a skill or a possibility. The interrogative sentence structure "能……吗（néng...ma）?" is often used to indicate a request or hope for permission. For example:

我能进来吗（wǒ néng jìn lái ma）？

May I come in?

明天下午我能过去（míng tiān xià wǔ wǒ néng guò qù）。

I can go there tomorrow in the afternoon.

会（huì）

It is used before a verb, indicating acquiring a skill through learning. Its negative form is 不会（bú huì）. For example:

他会说中文（tā huì shuō zhōng wén）。

He can speak Chinese.

我不会游泳（wǒ bú huì yóu yǒng）。

I cannot swim.

It also indicates the possibility of the situation mentioned. For example:

你会拉小提琴吗（nǐ huì lā xiǎo tí qín ma）？会（huì）。

Can you play the violin? –Yes, I can.

明天她会来吗（míng tiān tā huì lái ma）？她会来（tā huì lái）。

Will she come tomorrow? – Yes, she will.

Chinese modal verbs are similar to English modal verbs both in their function and meaning. They are usually not used by themselves but are joined by other verbs to function as predicates except in short answers. Semantically it is not difficult to find their English equivalents or approximations.

Adverbs are the words that modify verbs or adjectives by expressing time, scope, quality, state, or degree. For example: 不（bù），都（dōu），很（hěn），太（tài），etc. Adverbs do not modify nouns. Now, let's learn some adverbs together because they are really helpful for forming sentences.

才（cái）

It modifies a verb, giving the idea that some action or something has just happened. For example:

我才到（wǒ cái dào）。

I've just arrived.

他才离开（tā cái lí kāi）。

He has just left.

比较（bǐ jiào）

It may be used either as a verb or an adverb. When used as an adverb, it modifies adjectives or certain verbs, indicating that a quality or state of things has attained a certain degree. For example:

今天比较冷（jīn tiān bǐ jiào lěng）。

Today is much colder.

我比较喜欢动作片（wǒ bǐ jiào xǐ huān dòng zuò piàn）。

I prefer action movies.

都（dōu）

It is an adverb of scope. It means "all, in all cases", "with no exception." What is modified by it must be in the plural and placed before it. For example:

他们都是中国人（tā men dōu shì zhōng guó rén）。

They are all Chinese.

我们都喜欢喝茶（wǒ men dōu xǐ huān hē chá）。

We all like to drink tea.

很（hěn）

It is often used before an adjective or a verb expressing thought or emotion to denote degree. The usual pattern is "很（hěn）+ adjective/verb". Negation is achieved by adding 不（bù）before or after 很（hěn）, but different positions imply different degrees in negation. For example: 很不好（hěn bùhǎo）means very bad while 不很好（bú hěn hǎo）means not very good. For example:

他是一个很友好的人（tā shìyígè hěn yǒu hǎo de rén）。

He's a very friendly guy.

她的脾气很不好（tā de pí qì hěn bùhǎo）。

She has a very bad temper.

这家旅馆的环境不是很好（zhè jiā lǚ guǎn de huán jìng bú shì hěn hǎo）。

The environment of this hotel is not good.

When used in an affirmative sentence, it has only a weak sense, much weaker than the English adverb "very", which expresses a high degree of quality. Indeed, 很（hěn）is sometimes used for the sake of euphony, for without it the sentence may sound awkward. For example:

你的身体好（nǐ de shēn tǐ hǎo）。

你的身体很好（nǐ de shēn tǐ hěn hǎo）。

Both of the sentences mean "You are in good health." But the first sentence sounds strange and awkward to a native speaker.

可能（kě néng）

It expresses supposition or estimation. Occurring before a verb, an adjective, or the subject, it indicates that an action is likely to take place, an event or state of things is likely to happen or be in existence. The usual pattern is "……可能（kě néng）+ verb /adjective……". The negative form is 不可能（bú kě néng），which usually does not appear before the subject. For example:

他可能去图书馆了（tā kě néng qù tú shū guǎn le）。

He may have gone to the library.

我可能要出差（wǒ kě néng yào chū chāi）。

I may have a business trip.

非常（fēi cháng）

It modifies adjectives or certain verbs, indicating that a quality or state of things has attained a very high degree. For example:

今天非常热（jīn tiān fēi cháng rè）。Today is very hot.

我非常高兴（wǒ fēi cháng gāo xìng）。I'm very happy.

太（tài）

It indicates a high degree. 了（le）is often used at the end of the sentences with 太（tài），but not in negative sentences. For example:

天太热了（tiān tài rè le）。The weather is too hot.

我听不太懂（wǒ tīng bú tài dǒng）。I don't quite understand.

还（hái）

Used as an adverbial, it modifies a verb or an adjective. It expresses the repetition of an action, continuity of a state, the further development of an event, or it's reaching a higher degree. For example:

我下周还要出差（wǒ xià zhōu hái yào chū chāi）。

I still have a business trip next week.

冰箱里还有两个苹果（bīng xiāng lǐ hái yǒu liǎng gè píng guǒ）。

There are still two apples in the fridge.

没有/没（méi yǒu/ méi）

When occurring before a verb or an adjective, 没有/没（méi yǒu/ méi）denies that an action has already begun or a state of things has come into being. The usual pattern is "……没有/没（méi yǒu/ méi）+ verb/ adjective……" For example:

我没回家（wǒ méi huí jiā）。

I didn't go home.

昨天没有下雨（zuó tiān méi yǒu xià yǔ）。

Yesterday didn't rain.

经常/常常 (jīng cháng/ cháng cháng)

It modifies verbs, indicating a high frequency of an action. The negative form is 不常 (bùcháng).

我经常去图书馆 (wǒ jīng cháng qù tú shū guǎn)。

I often go to the library.

他不常出门 (tā bùcháng chū mén)。

He seldom goes out.

随时 (suí shí)

It is often used as an adverbial to modify a verb, indicating that the action may take place at any time, or regardless of time. For example:

我随时有空 (wǒ suí shí yǒu kòng)。

I'm free at any time.

欢迎随时来找我 (huān yíng suí shí lái zhǎo wǒ)。

(You're) welcome to visit me at any time.

在/正在 (zài/ zhèng zài)

When used before a verb, 在/正在 (zài / zhèng zài) are adverbs of time, denoting that an action is in progress. The usual pattern is "……在/正在 (zài / zhèng zài) + verb ……". If 不 (bù) occurs before 在 (zài), it is a negation. If 不 (bù) is placed before 正在 (zhèng zài), it forms a rhetorical question, making the meaning of the sentence affirmative. For example:

他在听歌，他不在学习 (tā zài tīng gē, tā bú zài xué xí)。

He's listening to the music; he's not studying.

她不正在唱歌 (tā bú zhèng zài chàng gē)?

Isn't she singing?

Generally speaking, the 在/不在（zài / bú zài）sentence pattern is approximate to the English progressive aspect. It may refer to the past, the present, or the future, the specific time being brought out by time-words or the context.

已经（yǐ jīng）

It is used to modify a verb or an adjective. It shows the completion of an action or that quality or state of things has reached a certain degree. For example:

我已经到了（wǒ yǐ jīng dào le）。

I've arrived.

演出已经开始了（yǎn chū yǐ jīng kāi shǐ le）。

The show has begun.

挺（tǐng）

It is often used as an adverbial to modify an adjective or a verb of thought or emotion, indicating that a quality or state of things has attained a high degree. This word is quite common in colloquial speech. For example:

我挺想你（wǒ tǐng xiǎng nǐ）。

I miss you very much.

这里的天挺蓝（zhè lǐ de tiān tǐng lán）。

The sky here is quite blue.

一直（yìzhí）

It often modifies a verb or an adjective as an adverbial. It indicates the continuity of an action or a state. For example:

他一直喜欢你（tā yìzhí xǐ huān nǐ）。

He always liked you.

商店一直营业到晚上十点（shāng diàn yìzhí yíng yè dào wǎn shàng shí diǎn）。

The store is open until 10 pm.

一定（yídìng）

When used before a verb or an adjective, it is an adverb. When in first person, 一定（yídìng）expresses a firm will on the part of the speaker. In second or third person, 一定（yídìng）denotes an urgent request by the speaker or a strong probability. There are usually 要（yào），会（huì），能（néng），etc. between 一定（yídìng）and a verb or adjective. For example:

我们一定会来接你（wǒ men yídìng huì lái jiē nǐ）。

We will surely come to pick you up.

你一定要听老师讲话（nǐ yídìng yào tīng lǎo shī jiǎng huà）。

You have to listen to your teacher.

一共（yígòng）

It expresses totality. It often modifies a verb or an adverbial to indicate a total sum. It is also sometimes joined directly with a quantity word. For example:

我一共买了三个苹果（wǒ yígòng mǎi le sān gè píng guǒ）。

I bought three apples in total.

四个苹果一共一千克（sì gè píng guǒ yígòng yī qiān kè）。

Four apples weigh 1kg in total.

一共多少钱（yígòng duō shǎo qián）？

How much in total?

The subject, the predicate, and the object

The subject in a Chinese sentence is the topic to talk about and the predicate tells how it is or what it is. The subject is usually a noun or a pronoun and the predicate, a verb or an adjective. The sentence element that is governed by a verb and denotes a person or thing affected by the action expressed by the verb is called an object. In Chinese sentences, an object is usually placed after a verb. Objects are often nouns or pronouns. Let's take an example and analyze it:

我们学习中文（wǒ men xué xí zhōng wén）。

We learn Chinese.

我们（wǒ men），a pronoun, is the subject; 学习（xué xí），a verb, is the predicate; 中文（zhōng wén），a noun, is the object. Pretty easy, right?

A sentence with a verb as its predicate is one in which a verb plays the part of the predicate. In such a sentence, the predicate expresses the action or behavior of the subject. A verb may or may not take an object. A sentence with a verb as its predicate is negated by using the negative adverb 不（bù）before the predicate verb. For example:

我们学习游泳（wǒ men xué xí yóu yǒng）。

We learn to swim.

我们不学习游泳（wǒ men bù xué xí yóu yǒng）。

We don't learn to swim.

我们（wǒ men），a pronoun, is the subject; 学习（xué xí），a verb, is the predicate; 游泳（yóu yǒng），a verb, is the object. Not hard, right?

Prepositions and the adverbial

Prepositions are words that are placed before nouns or pronouns and are used together with them to express the direction, object, time, place, etc. of an action. Prepositions and the nouns or pronouns following them form prepositional constructions. For example:

在（zài）

It combines with a noun or a phrase denoting time, place, or direction to form a prepositional construction which is used as an adverbial to express the time or place of an action. Negation is achieved by adding 不（bù）before 在（zài）. For example:

我在图书馆看书（wǒ zài tú shū guǎn kàn shū）。

I'm in the library reading a book.

我在医院工作（wǒ zài yī yuàn gōng zuò）。

I'm working in a hospital.

往（wǎng）

It is used with a noun or pronoun to form a prepositional construction which modifies a verb, showing the direction of an action. A prepositional construction with 往（wǎng）either precedes it as an adverbial or follows it as a complement. For example:

你再往前走五分钟就到了（nǐ zài wǎng qián zǒu wǔ fēn zhōng jiù dào le）。

You will arrive there by walking forward for another five minutes.

前往北京的航班将在五分钟后起飞（qián wǎng běi jīng de háng bān jiāng zài wǔ fēn zhōng hòu qǐ fēi）。

The flight to Beijing will depart in five minutes.

从（cóng）

It indicates a starting point. It is usually combined with a noun or nominal phrase that denotes time or place to form a prepositional construction. It is used as an adverbial modifying a verb by telling when or where the action starts. For example:

我从公园回来（wǒ cóng gōng yuán huí lái）。

I came back from the park.

她从去年开始学中文（tā cóng qù nián kāi shǐ xué zhōng wén）。

She's been learning Chinese since last year.

由（yóu）

It is usually combined with a noun or pronoun to form a prepositional construction. It is used as an adverbial modifying a verb showing the doer of the action. In a sentence with 由（yóu）introducing the doer, the subject is the receiver of the action. When the verb takes an object, there is a certain semantic relationship between the subject and the object. The usual pattern is "……由（yóu）+ noun/pronoun + verb…… ". It may be compared with the English preposition "by" and implies the passive voice. For example:

中文由我来教（zhōng wén yóu wǒ lái jiāo）。

I'll be teaching Chinese.

这项活动由我负责（zhè xiàng huó dòng yóu wǒ fù zé）。

This activity will be my responsibility.

向（xiàng）

The preposition 向（xiàng）and the noun or pronoun following it forms a prepositional construction that modifies a verb. It shows the direction in which an action goes. It may be used before a verb and acts as an adverbial, or after a verb and functions as a complement. For example:

图书馆向这边走，公园向那边走（tú shū guǎn xiàng zhè biān zǒu, gōng yuán xiàng nà biān zǒu）。

Go this way to the library and that way to the park.

Prepositional constructions with 向（xiàng）may also denote the object of an action, for example:

我向服务员要了发票（wǒ xiàng fú wù yuán yào le fā piào）。

I asked for the invoice from the waiter.

他向我借了一本书（tā xiàng wǒ jiè le yìběn shū）。

He borrowed a book from me.

When it denotes the direction in which an action goes, it is more or less equivalent to the English preposition "to" or "toward". However, when 向 (xiàng) refers to the object of an action, it is often equivalent to "from" in English.

和/跟 (hé /gēn)

When used as prepositions, they are combined with a noun or pronoun to form prepositional constructions, which are as adverbials modifying verbs. The prepositional constructions indicate the object of an action. 和 (hé) and 跟 (gēn) are similar in use. For example:

我已经和他说了这件事（wǒ yǐ jīng hé tā shuō le zhè jiàn shì）。

I've told him this thing.

她跟我说她喜欢我（tā gēn wǒ shuō tā xǐ huān wǒ）。

She told me that she liked me.

Adverbials are usually adverbs, adjectives, prepositional constructions, or some nouns denoting time or place. In Chinese, adverbials normally occur before the verbs or adjectives they modify. Adverbials expressing time, place, or scope are sometimes placed before subjects. For example:

我们都学中文（wǒ men dōu xué zhōng wén）。

We're all learning Chinese.

昨天下午，他在教室学习（zuó tiān xià wǔ, tā zài jiào shì xué xí）。

Yesterday afternoon, he was studying in the classroom.

In general, when speaking Chinese, we can divide different adverbials into time, place, degree, starting point, manner, direction, and object. Now, let's discuss them one by one.

When a time word serves as an adverbial modifier in a sentence, it expresses the time at which an action takes place or a state of things comes into existence. It may be an adverb, a noun denoting time, or a time-phrase. It often follows the subject. Sometimes it can be used before the subject, a verb, or an adjective. For example:

我下周去中国（wǒ xià zhōu qù zhōng guó）。

I will go to China next week.

他下午两点来接你（tā xià wǔ liǎng diǎn lái jiē nǐ）。

He will pick you up at 2pm.

上个月我请假了（shàng gè yuè wǒ qǐng jiǎ le）。

I asked for days off last month.

An adverbial of place shows where an action takes place. It is often a prepositional construction or a noun denoting place. For example:

我在公园散步（wǒ zài gōng yuán sàn bù）。

I'm in the park walking.

我在床上看书（wǒ zài chuáng shàng kàn shū）。

I'm on the bed reading.

An adverbial of degree indicates the degree that a quality or state of things has attained. It is usually an adverb and modifies an adjective or a verb of thought or emotion. For example:

他最喜欢踢足球（tā zuì xǐ huān tī zú qiú）。

He likes to play soccer the most.

她很热情（tā hěn rè qíng）。

She is really welcoming.

An adverbial of starting point expresses the beginning of an action in time, space, or number. It is usually a prepositional construction. For example:

他从美国来（tā cóng měi guó lái）。

He comes from America.

电影从晚上七点开始（diàn yǐng cóng wǎn shàng qī diǎn kāi shǐ）。

The movie starts at seven in the evening

An adverbial of manner shows the way in which an action is carried out. It is usually an adjective or adverb. For example:

我们一起学习中文（wǒ men yìqǐ xué xí zhōng wén）。

We're learning Chinese together.

他们都推荐你（tā men dōu tuī jiàn nǐ）。

They all recommend you.

An adverbial of direction tells the direction in which an action progresses. It is usually a construction with a preposition. For example:

往前走就是机场（wǎng qián zǒu jiù shì jī chǎng）。

Keep going forward, and there will be the airport.

由北京前来的航班将在五分钟抵达（yóu běi jīng qián lái de háng bān jiāng zài wǔ fèn zhōng dǐ dá）。

The flight from Beijing will arrive in five minutes.

An adverbial of object tells the object of an action or the doer of an action. It is usually a prepositional construction with prepositions such as 向（xiàng） and 由（yóu）. For example:

他不停向我挥手（tābùtíng xiàng wǒ huī shǒu）。

He constantly waves to me.

最后一个节目由她出演（zuì hòu yígèjiémù yóu tā chū yǎn）。

She'll be performing in the last show.

Conjunction, particle, and the attribute

Conjunctions are the words that connect words, phrases, or clauses and by doing so, express the relationships between them. Let's learn some words here.

和/跟/与（hé/ gēn/ yǔ）

They are used to connect two or more elements, indicating a parallel relationship. When more than two items are connected, they can be used only between the last two items. For example:

桌子上有一本书和一杯水（zhuō zǐ shàng yǒu yì běn shū héyì bēi shuǐ）。

There is a book and a cup of water on the table.

我喜欢吃香蕉、苹果和西瓜（wǒ xǐ huān chī xiāng jiāo, píng guǒ hé xī guā）。

I like to eat banana, apple, and watermelon.

我与他相处不好（wǒ yǔ tāxiāng chǔ bùhǎo）。

I'm not getting along well with him.

Particles are words that are added to words, phrases, or sentences to express additional meaning. Chinese particles fall into three groups: structural particles, aspect particles, and modal particles. Let's take some examples.

吗（ma）

The particle 吗 (ma) indicates an interrogative mood. When 吗 (ma) is added at the end of a declarative sentence, the sentence turns into a question. For example:

你是美国人吗（nǐ shì měi guó rén ma）?

Are you an American?

你喜欢这首歌吗（nǐ xǐ huān zhè shǒu gē ma）?

Do you like this song?

的/地/得 (de)

When the structural particle 的 (de) is attached to a noun, a verb, an adjective, or a word of other parts of speech, they enter into what is called "a construction with 的 (de)". Such a construction is equivalent to a noun both in nature and function. For example:

他是我的老师（tā shì wǒ de lǎo shī）。

He's my teacher.

这是她的书（zhè shì tā de shū）。

This is her book.

There are similar constructions in English. When the 的 (de) construction is made up of a noun and 的 (de), it is like the independent genitive (the genitive without a headword) in English. For example:

这本书是我的（zhè běn shū shì wǒ de）。

This book is mine.

这只铅笔不是你的（zhè zhī qiān bǐ bú shì nǐ de）。

This pencil is not yours.

When the construction is made up of an adjective and 的 (de), it is like an adjective plus the prop-word "one." For example:

他的外套是新的（tā de wài tào shì xīn de）。

His coat is a new one.

When a verb enters into a 的 (de) construction, though comparable with a non-finite verb modifying the prop-word "one", it is better to turn the Chinese sentence into an English sentence with the predicate verb in the passive voice. For example:

那本小说是从图书馆借来的（nà běn xiǎo shuō shì cóng tú shū guǎn jiè lái de）。

That novel was borrowed from the library.

When 的 (de) is at the end of a sentence, it expresses affirmation. For example:

你会好起来的（nǐ huì hǎo qǐ lái de）。

You will recover.

我会来接你的（wǒ huì lái jiē nǐ de）。

I will pick you up.

地 (de) is used before a verb or an adjective to show that what precedes it is an adverbial modifying the verb or the adjective. As a rule, a disyllabic adjective or a monosyllabic adjective with an adverb of degree before it calls for the use of the particle 地 (de).

飞机安全地着陆了（fēi jī ān quán de zhuólù le）。

The plane landed safely.

她开心地走了（tā kāi xīn de zǒu le）。

She left happily.

得 (de) is used after a verb or an adjective to show that the following element is a complement to the verb or the adjective. Complements of degree or result are usually preceded by 得 (de). For example:

他跑得很快（tā pǎo de hěn kuài）。

He runs fast.

我的中文说得很流利（wǒ de zhōng wén shuō de hěn liú lì）。

I can speak Chinese fluently.

……的话（de huà）

It is a modal particle of assumption. Occurring at the end of a clause, 的话（de huà）indicates that what is said is an assumption. For example:

他还不来的话我就走（tā hái bù lái de huà wǒ jiù zǒu）。

I'll leave if he still doesn't show up.

不出意外的话我们马上就到了（bù chū yì wài de huà wǒ men mǎ shàng jiù dào le）。

We'll be there shortly unless something unexpected happens.

呢（ne）

It is used after a noun or pronoun, forming a question about the situation mentioned previously. The commonly used sentence pattern is A…B呢（ne）? For example:

我今天很好，你呢（wǒ jīn tiān hěn hǎo, nǐ ne）?

I'm fine today; how about you?

你呢（nǐ ne） means 你今天好吗（nǐ jīn tiān hǎo ma） in this context.

It can also ask about the location of somebody or something. For example:

我的钱包呢（wǒ de qián bāo ne）?

Where is my wallet?

她在哪儿呢（tā zài nǎ ér ne）？

Where is she?

When placed after a declarative sentence, it means that the action is just going on. It is often used in conjunction with adverbs like 在/正在（zài / zhèng zài）. For example:

她在跳舞呢（tā zài tiào wǔ ne）。

She's dancing right now.

我在睡觉呢（wǒ zài shuì jiào ne）。

I'm sleeping.

吧（ba）

When used at the end of an imperative sentence, it indicates suggestion or command with a softened mood. For example:

我们在这家餐厅吃饭吧（wǒ men zài zhè jiā cān tīng chī fàn ba）。

Let's eat at this restaurant.

他不在这，你等会再来吧（tā bú zài zhè, nǐ děng huì zài lái ba）。

He's not here; you can come back later.

When used at the end of an interrogative sentence, it indicates supposition. Questions with 吧（ba）at the end are similar to English disjunctive questions spoken with a falling tone. For example:

这本书是你的吧（zhè běn shū shì nǐ de ba）？

This book is yours, isn't it?

啊（ā）

It is used at the end of a declarative sentence to set the mood. The pronunciations of 啊 (ā) varies with the finals of the syllables before it, and in written Chinese, the variants are represented by different characters sometimes. For example:

这里真美啊（zhè lǐ zhēn měi ā）！

What a beautiful place!

这座山真高啊（zhè zuò shān zhēn gāo ā）！

This mountain is so tall!

了 (le)

了 (le) is used at the end of a sentence to indicate a change or the occurrence of a new situation or completion. For example:

你的朋友来了（nǐ de péng yǒu lái le）。

Your friend has arrived.

他一会就要走了（tā yī huì jiù yào zǒu le）。

He will leave soon.

了 (le) can be also be used between a verb and its object. There is usually a modifier before the object of the verb such as a numeral classifier, an adjective, or a pronoun, etc, For example:

她买了几个苹果（tā mǎi le jǐ gè píng guǒ）。

She bought a few apples.

你看见了几个人（nǐ kàn jiàn le jǐ gè rén）？

How many people have you seen?

The negative form of 了 (le) in both cases above is 没 (méi) + verb + object. In the negative form, 了 (le) should be omitted. For example:

你的朋友没来（nǐ de péng yǒu méi lái）。

Your friend hasn't come.

她没买苹果（tā méi mǎi píng guǒ）。

She didn't buy the apple.

过（guò）

Used after a verb, the aspect particle 过（guò）indicates that the action took place in the past and ended before the present time or that there was such an experience. The usual pattern is "...verb + 过（guò）..." Negation is achieved by adding 没（méi）or 没有（méi yǒu）before the verb, For example:

我吃过饭了（wǒ chī guò fàn le）。

I've eaten already.

我没去过美国（wǒ méi qù guò měi guó）。

I've never been to America.

Both aspect particles, 过（guò）and 了（le）indicate an action which takes place before a certain moment. 过（guò）emphasizes the completion of an action and often implies a reference to that moment whereas 了（le）only indicates a prior experience. Therefore, in most cases, a verb with 过（guò）is comparable with English perfect tense and verbs with 了（le）are comparable with simple past tense.

着（zhe）

When used after a verb, 着（zhe）indicates that the action is in progress or remains unchanged. No word can be inserted between the verb and 着（zhe）. For example:

他正在看着一本漫画书（tā zhèng zài kàn zhe yì běn màn huà shū）。

He is currently reading a comic book.

他们在热烈的讨论着什么东西（tā men zài rè liè de tǎo lùn zhe shén me dōng xī）。

They're fiercely discussing something.

The attribute is usually a noun, a pronoun, an adjective, a numeral, or a measure word. In Chinese, an attribute is as a rule placed before a noun which it modifies. Such a noun is called the "headword". The structural particle 的（de）is often used between a noun and its headword. For example:

我的朋友是老师（wǒ de péng yǒu shì lǎo shī）。

My friend is a teacher. "我的（wǒ de）" is the attribute here.

她是一个好学生（tā shì yí gè hǎo xué shēng）。

She's a good student. "一个（yí gè）" is the attribute here.

Note here, attributes in Chinese sentences, whether they are words, phrases or clauses, are almost invariable placed before headwords. The particle 的（de）is a sign of an attribute. It may be used after a word, phrase, or clause to make it an attribute, but numerals and demonstrative pronouns do not need 的（de）when they function as attributes. When a noun is modified by a series of attributes, 的（de）can be used after each attribute.

Restrictive attributes express the time, number, possession, etc. of the persons or things spoken of, telling whose, when, where, how many, how much they are. For example:

这是我的钢笔，那是他的钢笔（zhè shì wǒ de gāng bǐ, nà shì tā de gāng bǐ）。

This is my pen, and that is his pen.

她没去看昨天的电影（tā méi qù kàn zuó tiān de diàn yǐng）。

She didn't go see yesterday's movie.

Position words and construction with position words

Position words are the words that indicate direction or position. They are a subclass of noun. There are two types of them: simple position words such as 上（shàng）, 下（xià）, 里（lǐ）and compound words such as 上面（shàng miàn）, 下面（xià miàn）, 里面（lǐ miàn）.

Position words may be attached to other words to form constructions with position words, e.g. 楼上（lóu shàng）, 床下（chuáng xià）, 假期里（jiǎ qī lǐ）, 房间内（fáng jiān nèi）.

Position words are a special class of nouns in Chinese. They usually express the location (either in time or space) of things. Very often they are equivalent to English prepositions, e.g. 房间里（fáng jiān lǐ）— in the room, 桌子下（zhuō zǐ xià）— under the table, 礼堂外（lǐ táng wài）— outside of auditorium, 报纸上（bào zhǐ shàng）— on the newspaper. A Chinese position word does not always equal an English preposition. For example, position words may be used alone to serve as a sentence element. Constructions with position words sometimes act like prepositional phrases and sometimes do not; they may perform the function of a subject whereas English prepositional phrases can never be a subject. For example:

楼下有个小卖部（lóu xià yǒu gè xiǎo mài bù）。

There is a small store downstairs.

房间里很热（fáng jiān lǐ hěn rè）。

It's hot in the room.

In the two sentences, "楼上（lóu shàng）" and "房间里（fáng jiān lǐ）" are the constructions with position words acting as the subject but "downstairs" and "in the room" are not.

Now, let's discuss some position words together. They're sure to be very useful.

里 (lǐ) and 外 (wài) are both both position words but with opposite meanings. 里 (lǐ) means in or inside something while 外 (wài) means outside something, For example:

商场里东西很多（shāng chǎng lǐ dōng xī hěn duō）。

There are lots of things in the mall.

他的家在城市外（tā de jiā zài chéng shì wài）。

He lives outside the city.

As a position word, 来/以来 (lái /yǐ lái) is used a word or expression denoting a period of time. It denotes the duration from a point of time in the past to the time of speaking. For example:

这几年以来，我去过很多地方（zhè jǐ nián yǐ lái, wǒ qù guò hěn duō dì fāng）。

During recent years, I've been to many places.

Compound position words are made up of simple position words and 之 (zhī) or 以 (yǐ) which precedes them or simple position words and 面 (miàn)，边（biān），or 头 (tóu) which follows them.

Though usually adverbials, constructions with position words may also act as subjects. In sentences with such subjects, the predicates are either adjectives or verbs of existence. For example:

俱乐部里有放映厅（jù lè bù lǐ yǒu fàng yìng tīng）。

There is a projection room in the club.

公园里有很多人（gōng yuán lǐ yǒu hěn duō rén）。

There are a lot of people inthe park.

房间里很整洁（fáng jiān lǐ hěn zhěng jié）。

The room is clean and tidy.

Just to remember: the Chinese sentence which has a position word construction as subject and a verb of existence as predicate is equal in meaning to the English sentence "There + to be + subject + adverbial." When the predicate is an adjective instead of a verb of existence, the sentence is similar to the English SVC verb patterns, the noun in the position word construction functioning as the subject.

The complement and the independent element

The complement is a supplementary or explanatory element which is attached to a verb or an adjective. It indicates how the action is going on, what the result is, how many times or how long it is done, or what degree or extent a quality or state of things reaches. It is usually an adjective, an adverb, or a verb. Now, we'll discuss a complement of result, number, manner, degree, direction, and possibility here.

A complement of result tells the result of an action. It is usually a verb or an adjective. For example:

我们已经看完了电影（wǒ men yǐ jīng kàn wán le diàn yǐng）。

We have finished watching the movie.

你说什么我听不清楚（nǐ shuō shénme wǒ tīng bùqīng chǔ）。

What are you saying? I can't hear you clearly.

The complement of number tells how many times an action takes place or how long it lasts. It is usually a quantity word. For example:

我还想多睡一会儿（wǒ hái xiǎng duō shuìyìhuì ér）。

I still want to sleep for a while.

再等我五分钟（zài děng wǒ wǔ fēn zhōng）。

Just wait for me for another five minutes.

In many cases, Chinese complements are similar (in meaning) to English adverbials. A complement of numbers functions in Chinese sentences as adverbials of time in English sentences.

The complement of manner tells how an action takes place. For example:

请你讲慢一点（qǐng nǐ jiǎng màn yìdiǎn）。

Please speak slowly.

你能开车开快一点吗?我要迟到了（nǐ néng kāi chē kāi kuài yìdiǎn ma? wǒ yào chí dào le）。

Can you drive faster? I'll be late.

A complement of degree tells the degree that a quality or state of things has reached. It is usually an adverb or adjective. For example:

我身体很好（wǒ shēn tǐ hěn hǎo）。

I'm in good health.

他是一个挺不错的人（tā shìyígè tǐng bú cuò de rén）。

He is quite a nice guy.

The completion of direction tells the direction of an action or a state. In this case, a directional verb often occurs after another verb or an adjective. For example:

她送来了水果和蛋糕（tā sòng lái le shuǐ guǒ hé dàn gāo）。

She bring usfruits and cakes.

他向你走过来了（tā xiàng nǐ zǒu guò lái le）。

He comes over to you.

The complement of possibility tells the possibility of an action taking place or being realized. It is usually a verb or an adjective. Negation is formed by adding 不（bù）after the predicate verb.

路程不远，我们今天能赶到（lù chéng bù yuǎn, wǒ men jīn tiān néng gǎn dào）。

It's not far; we can make it today.

现在我没空，去不了（xiàn zài wǒ méi kōng, qù bù liǎo）。

I'm not available now; I cannot go there.

An independent element in a sentence is one which has no structural relation with other elements and is rather flexible in word position. It may be a vocative, an echo, an interjection, or a reminder. It may also be used to express supposition, affirmation, emphasis, etc. All in all, it will help your fluency greatly. For example:

看你，又忘了吧，我不喜欢喝可乐 （kàn nǐ, yòu wàng le ba, wǒ bù xǐ huān hē kě lè）。

Look at you, you forgot again? I don't like coke.

哎呀，我们好久不见了（ài ya, wǒ men hǎo jiǔ bú jiàn le）。

Ah, we haven't seen each other in such a long time.

A brief introduction to other language points

Chinese has a lot of different kinds of sentence structures. Up to now in this chapter, I think our readers might feel bored from learning the grammar and have so many things to digest already. So, we will only introduce some very basic grammar for sentences here. Frankly speaking, you can even forget all the grammar mentioned in this book. Just remember the examples, keep learning different words, make your own examples, and you will get there finally.

Declarative sentences and interrogative sentences

A declarative sentence is a statement or an assertion. It is spoken with a flat tone. An interrogative sentence is a question. It is spoken with the tail rising. There are several types of Chinese interrogative sentences: yes-no questions, special questions, alternative questions, and affirmative/negative questions.

Chinese yes-no questions are equivalent to English general questions, but their formation is much simpler. Any Chinese declarative sentence can be turned into a yes-no question simply by adding 吗（ma）at its end.

In forming Chinese special questions, no inversion of any kind is required. Interrogative pronouns may be placed either at the head of a sentence, or at its end, or within the sentence, the position depending on the grammatical function of the interrogative pronoun. If it acts as a subject, it occupies the position of a subject; if it is used as an object, it takes the position of an object, etc. So, the word order of a special question is the same as that of a normal declarative sentence. This goes to show that word order in Chinese is sometimes quite rigid.

Elliptical sentence

Some sentence elements may be omitted in certain contexts in Chinese. For example:

谁在唱歌?她（shuí zài chàng gē? tā）。

Who's singing? She is.

今天去图书馆了吗?去了（jīn tiān qù tú shū guǎn le ma? qù le）。

Have you been to the library today? (I've) been there.

In the above sentence, the words "在唱歌（zài chàng gē）" and "图书馆（tú shū guǎn）" are omitted.

Pivotal sentence

In some Chinese sentences, the predicate consists of two verbs（or a verb and an adjective）in succession and the object of the first verb is at the same time the subject of the following verb（or adjective）. Such sentences are called pivotal sentences. The first verb in such a sentence is often a causative verb which calls forth an action indicated by the second verb. For example:

我们请她唱中文歌（wǒ men qǐng tā chàng zhōng wén gē）。

We asked her to sing Chinese songs.

老师要我按时交作业（lǎo shī yào wǒ àn shí jiāo zuò yè）。

The teacher told me to hand in the homework on time.

Like the examples above, the bulk of Chinese pivotal sentences are similar to English sentences with accusative-with-infinitive constructions (e.g. to allow/ask/command /force /order/persuade /request /tell somebody to do something).

Other pivotal sentences are comparable to English sentences with verb + object + particle/noun/adjective/adverbial, etc. For example:

她辅导我学中文（tā fǔ dǎo wǒ xué zhōng wén）。

She coached me in Chinese.

他们选你当俱乐部主席（tā men xuǎn nǐ dāng jù lè bù zhǔ xí）。

They voted you chairman of the club.

The verb 有（yǒu）may be used in a pivotal sentence. It is usually placed before the pivotal verb. Many of the pivotal sentences with the verb 有（yǒu）are without a subject. For example:

有个人来找你（yǒu gè rén lái zhǎo nǐ）。

There's someone looking for you.

周末有很多人去公园（zhōu mò yǒu hěn duō rén qù gōng yuán）。

There are a lot of people going to the park during the weekend.

The verb 祝（zhù） may be used in a pivotal sentence expressing good wishes. It is used to offer congratulations or when bidding farewell. Sentences with 祝（zhù）are sometimes without a subject. For example:

祝我好运吧（zhù wǒ hǎo yùn ba）。

Wish me good luck.

祝贺你（zhù hè nǐ）！

Congratulations!

Actions in the past

As mentioned earlier, Chinese verbs need not change according to the tense.

Actions in the past time or past experiences are expressed by using an adverbial of time before the verb or the aspect particle 过（guò）after the verb or both. The pattern is "...adverbial of time + verb + 过（guò）..." For example:

这本书他已经看过了（zhè běn shū tā yǐ jīng kàn guò le）。

He's already read this book.

她去年来过一次中国（tā qù nián lái guòyícì zhōng guó）。

She went to China once last year.

The negative form is "...adverbial of time + 没（méi）+ verb + 过（guò）..." For example:

她昨天没回过家（tā zuó tiān méi huí guò jiā）。

She didn't come back home yesterday.

Completed actions

The aspect particle 了（le）, or a complement of result, or both of them are used to show that an action has been completed or that something has been realized. The pattern is "...verb + complement of result + 了（le）". For example:

她已经写完作业了（tā yǐ jīng xiě wán zuò yè le）。

She's already finished her homework.

他已经回来了（tā yǐ jīng huí lái le）。

He's already come back.

The completion of an action indicates a stage that the action has reached. It has no relevance to time. An action, whether it took place in the past, is taking place now, or will take place in the future, must have its stage of completion. But when translating into English, we don't need to use the corresponding tense. For example:

他昨天去了公园（tā zuó tiān qù le gōng yuán）。

He went to the park yesterday.

明天我们下了班就去看电影（míng tiān wǒ men xià le bān jiù qù kàn diàn yǐng）。

We'll go to the cinema after we get off work tomorrow.

Progressive aspect of an action

A verb may take an adverbial of time before it, or the aspect particle 着 (zhe) after it or both, to show that the action referred to is in progress or that an event remains what it has been. For example:

他在练习说中文（tā zài liàn xí shuō zhōng wén）。

He's practicing speaking Chinese.

外面下着大雨（wài miàn xià zhe dà yǔ）。

It's raining heavily outside.

The progressive aspect of an action denotes a state that the action is in. It has no relation with time. Almost any action has a progressive aspect regardless of the time of its happening. For example:

我们明天带着相机去吧（wǒ men míng tiān dài zhe xiàng jī qù ba）。

Let's take a camera there tomorrow.

昨天晚上窗户一直开着（zuó tiān wǎn shàng chuāng hù yìzhí kāi zhe）。

The window was open the whole night yesterday.

Focus here. In English, of course you can say, "He's dying out there," but in Chinese, there is no such expression.

Affirmative + negative question

An affirmative + negative question is one which is formed by placing the affirmation and negation of the predicate verb or adjective side by side. For example:

你有没有学过中文（nǐ yǒu méi yǒu xué guò zhōng wén）？

Have you studied Chinese or not?

你信不信我（nǐ xìn bú xìn wǒ）？

Do you believe me or not?

If the verb takes an object, the object may be placed between the affirmative and negative forms of the verb. This makes you speak much more like a native speaker. The first sentence of the above examples above may be turned to:

你有学过中文没（nǐ yǒu xué guò zhōng wén méi）？

The affirmative + negative questions can be considered as a special kind of yes-no questions. They have the same meaning as yes-no questions but are more colloquial in style.

The apposition

When two words or expressions in a sentence stand for the same person or thing and perform the same grammatical function, with one explaining or denoting the other, then the former is said to be in apposition to the latter. The two words or expressions are sometimes placed side-by-side, and sometimes one is at the head of a sentence whereas the other occurs in the middle of the sentence. The one that occurs in the middle is usually a pronoun. For example:

中国、美国，这两个国家的风景都很美丽（zhōng guó, měi guó, zhè liǎng gè guó jiā de fēng jǐng dōu hěn měi lì）。

China and America, both of them have beautiful landscapes.

香蕉、苹果和橘子，它们都是我爱吃的水果（xiāng jiāo, píng guǒ hé jú zǐ, tā men dōu shì wǒ ài chī de shuǐ guǒ）。

Banana, apple and orange, they are all fruits I love eating.

A special feature of Chinese apposition is that pronouns may be in apposition to nouns. In sentences above, the pronoun 这 (zhè) and 它们 (tā men) may be omitted; without them, the sentences still stand. The use of pronouns as apposition is often colloquial in style; sometimes it could be emotional as one may find in lyrics.

Sentence with two objects

In some sentences, the predicate verb affects two objects and therefore takes two objects. For example:

他问我一个问题（tā wèn wǒ yígè wèn tí）。

He asked me a question.

她教你们中文（tā jiāo nǐ men zhōng wén）。

She teaches you Chinese.

Of the two objects, the first, 我 (wǒ), 你们 (nǐ men) in the above examples, which refers to persons, are called indirect objects, or the near object. The second objects such as 问题 (wèn tí), 中文 (zhōng wén) in the above examples, refers to things and are called the direct object, or the far object.

Sentence with an adjectival predicate

Used in the structure subject + adverb of degree + adjective, the adjective describes the nature or state of somebody or something, usually following the adverb of degree 很 (hěn). The negative form is subject + 不 (bù) + adjective. For example:

我很好 (wǒ hěn hǎo)。

I'm very good.

她的中文不好 (tā de zhōng wén bù hǎo)。

Her Chinese is not very good.

Sentence with a nominal predicate

It is a sentence whose predicate is a nominal element. It is usually used to indicate age, time, date, etc. For example:

明天星期一 (míng tiān xīng qī yī)。

Tomorrow is Monday.

我今年二十五岁 (wǒ jīn nián èr shí wǔ suì)。

I'm twenty-five years old this year.

Sentence with a serial verb construction

去/来 (qù / lái) + place + to do sth

The predicate of a sentence with a serial verb construction consists of two or more verbs. The latter verb can be the purpose of the former. The object of the first verb, i.e. the place, can sometimes be omitted. For example:

我们去中国看大熊猫 (wǒ men qù zhōng guó kàn dà xióng māo)。

We're going to China to look at pandas.

她来公园散步 (tā lái gōng yuán sàn bù)。

She comes to the park to take a walk.

Sentence with a subject-predicate phrase as the predicate

In Chinese, there is a kind of sentence in which the predicate is a subject predicate phrase. The structure is subject of sentence + predicate of the sentence/subject + predicate. For example:

我身体不太舒服（wǒ shēn tǐ bú tài shū fú）。

I don't feel well.

我牙疼（wǒ yá téng）。

My tooth aches.

The subject in the subject-predicate phrase is usually part of the subject of the sentence related to it.

Sentence with verbal expressions in series

A sentence with verbal expressions in series is one in which the predicate consists of two or more verbs (with or without an adjective) to tell something about the same subject. In speech, there is no pause between the verbs. There are various relationships between the verbs. Apart form 来 (lái) and 去 (qù); these verbs are usually not used alone, but with some other elements. For example:

我要去饭店吃晚饭（wǒ yào qù fàn diàn chī wǎn fàn）。

I want to go to the restaurant for dinner.

她用中文唱歌（tā yòng zhōng wén chàng gē）。

She uses Chinese to sing.

Verbal expressions in series are a syntactic peculiarity of Chinese sentences. This are possible because Chinese tends to use verbs and Chinese verbs have no non-finite forms.

The verbal expressions in series may have various relationships between them. They may be coordinate (the action referred to by the first verb preceding the others.) They may have a principal-subordinate relationship (one of the verbs denoting purpose, condition, manner, time, place, etc.) Therefore verbal expressions in series are comparable to English coordinate verbs, or a predicate verb with a a non-finite verb, or a predicate verb with an adverbial.

Sentences with 是（shì）

The 是（shì） sentence is a determinable sentence with 是（shì）, indicating what somebody or something equals or belongs to. It is expressed by "noun / pronoun + 是（shì）+ noun / pronoun". The negative sentence is formed by adding the negative adverb 不（bù）before 是（shì）, for example:

我是中国人（wǒ shì zhōng guó rén）。

I am a Chinese.

我不是中国人（wǒ bú shì zhōng guó rén）。

I am not a Chinese.

The Chinese sentence pattern "noun / pronoun + 是(shì) + noun / pronoun" is equal to the English sentence pattern "subject + link verb + complement". Negation is achieved by putting 不（bù）before 是（shì）while in the English sentence the negative particle "not" is placed after the link verb.

The structure 是……的 （shì... de） is used to emphasize time, place, or manner. When the occurrence of something is known, it can be use to emphasize when, where, and in which manner it occurred. 是 （shì）can be omitted in positive and interrogative sentences, but not in negative sentences. For example:

我是昨天来的（wǒ shì zuó tiān lái de）。

I came here yesterday.

这是在图书馆借的（zhè shì zài tú shū guǎn jiè de）。

This was borrowed from the library.

他不是昨天来的（tā bú shì zuó tiān lái de）。

He didn't arrive yesterday.

Composite sentence

Chinese composite sentences fall into two types: compound and complex. In a compound sentence, the component clauses are equal in importance, and there is no subordination in meaning. A complex sentence is generally made up of two clauses: one of them expresses the main idea of the sentence and is called the principal clause, and the other modifies or restricts the meaning of the principal clause and is called the subordinate clause.

Compound sentences may involve coordination, sequence, progression, alternation, etc. Complex sentences may have clauses of transition, supposition, condition, cause, etc.

The various relations between clauses are often indicated by words that are used to connect clauses. These words are called correlative words, e.g. 是……还是（shì... hái shì ），which indicates alternation; 不但……而且（bú dàn... ér qiě）which indicates progression; 如果……就（rú guǒ... jiù ），which indicates condition. For example:

你是美国人还是英国人（nǐ shì měi guó rén hái shì yīng guó rén）?

Are you an American or a British?

她不但会唱歌，还会跳舞（tā bú dàn huì chàng gē, hái huì tiào wǔ）。

She can not only sing but also dance. 如果明天下雨，我们就呆在家里（rú guǒ míng tiān xià yǔ, wǒ men jiù dāi zài jiā lǐ）。

If it rains tomorrow, we'll stay at home.

While English complex sentences normally need conjunctions to connect clauses, Chinese complex sentences may go without correlative words. This is true particularly in spoken Chinese. For example:

你不去我去（nǐ bú qù wǒ qù）。

If (or since) you won't go, I'll go.

他昨天病了，没去上课（tā zuó tiān bìng le, méi qù shàng kè）。

He was absent from class because he was ill.

Chapter 3: How to Count

Numbers are widely used in Chinese people's daily lives. It will bring inconvenience if they are used and spoken incorrectly. Luckily, the Chinese numerical system is fairly straightforward and logical. Once you have learned the first eleven numbers, you will be able to count from 0 to 99.

Below you will find the numbers zero to ten. Please make sure to practice saying each number using the correct tone.

Zero: 零, líng

One: 一, yī

Two: 二, èr

Three: 三, sān

Four: 四, sì

Five: 五, wǔ

Six: 六, liù

Seven: 七, qī

Eight: 八, bā

Nine: 九, jiǔ

Ten: 十, shí

Once you have mastered the numbers zero to ten, you can continue counting in double digits by saying the number in the tens' position, then the word 十 (shí), followed by the number in the one's position. For example: The number 48 is written and spoken as 四十八 (sì shí bā). The number 30 is written and spoken as 三十 (sān shí), the number 19 is written and spoken as 一十九 (yī shí jiǔ) or just 十九 (shí jiǔ)

The word for hundred in Chinese is 百 (bǎi), so 100 is spoken as 一百 (yìbǎi), 200 is spoken as 二百 (èrbǎi), 300 is spoken as 三百 (sānbǎi), etc.

Once you have mastered the word 百 (bǎi), you can continue counting all triple digits by saying the number in the hundreds' position, then the word 百 (bǎi, followed by saying the number in the tens' position, then the word 十 (shí), followed by the number in the one's position. For example:

The number 148 is written and spoken as 一百四十八 (yìbǎisì shí bā). The number 230 is written and spoken as 二百三十 (èr bǎisān shí), the number 319 is written and spoken as 三百一十九 (sān bǎiyī shí jiǔ). Attention, you cannot omit the 一 (yī) here. Additionally, numbers like 401, 502, etc, are written and spoken as 四百零一 (sìbǎiling yī), 五百零二 (wǔbǎiling èr), etc.

There is also 千 (qiān) for thousand, 万 (wàn) for ten thousand, 亿 (yì) for a hundred million. Just imagine how hard pronouncing 235,442,251 is in English! In Chinese, it's 二亿三千五百四十四万二千二百五十一 (èr yì sān wǔbǎisì shí sì wàn èr qiān èr bǎiwǔ shí yī).

Another thing that may be of interest, 两 (liǎng) is used for two when counting people and things, it can be also used as the first digit in two hundred (两百), two thousand (两千), etc, but only for the first digit. For example, 222 people can be spoken as 两百二十二人 (liǎng bǎièr shí èr rén) or 二百二十二人 (èr bǎièr shí èr rén).

Ordinal numbers are formed by adding 第 (dì) before the number. For example, 第一 (dì yī) means 1st, 第二 (dì èr) means 2nd, etc. 第 (dì) is sometimes omitted in numbers designating the order in a sequence, e.g. 二楼 (èr lóu) equals 第二楼 (dì èr lóu), the second floor.

The names for the twelve months in a year are formed by adding the suffix 月 (yuè) after the number: 一月 (yī yuè), 二月 (èr yuè) ... It is same for expressing the week. By using the prefix 星期 (xīng qī) or 周 (zhōu) before the number, you then can say all of them. The one exception is for Sunday. In oral Chinese, native speakers use 周天 (zhōu tiān) or 星期天 (xīng qī tiān) instead of 周七 (zhōu qī) or 星期七 (xīng qīqī). You can also express the names for days in a month by adding the suffix 日 (rì) or 号 (hào) after the number. For year, you can use the suffix 年 (nián) after numbers, for example: 2019年 (èr líng yī jiǔ nián). Compared with English, this is really easy to remember, right? If you're able to memorize the numbers, you should be able to say anything above.

In the telephone numbers, room numbers and bus/car numbers, the numeral 1 is often pronounced as yāo so as to clearly distinguish yī from qī.

In Chinese, a numeral does not modify a noun directly, but is followed by a measure word. Nouns have their proper measure words to go with, e.g. 一个人 (yí gè rén), 两条狗 (liǎng tiáo gǒu), 三辆车 (sān liàng chē) which means one person, two dogs, and three cars. Frankly speaking, this causes much headache for learners. Measure words have to be learned together with each individual noun. However, there is a general measure word 个 (gè) which is applicable to almost every individual noun. In case you are not sure which measure word goes with a certain noun, you may use 个 (gè) as a substitute. This way, your Chinese will not be so idiomatic, but it is better than not to use a measure word at all.

Fun facts:

Sometimes in written Chinese, numbers can represent certain phrases because they sound similar. For example:

521. Don't say "wǔbǎi èr shí yī" here, just "wǔ èr yī"; it sounds similar to 我爱你 (wǒ ài nǐ), which means "I love you".

518. Don't say "wǔbǎi yī shí bā" here, just "wǔ yāo bā"; it sounds similar to 我要发 (wǒ yào fā), which means "I'll be rich".

1314. Don't say "yī qiān sān bǎi yī shí sì" here, just "yī sān yī sì"; it sounds similar to 一生一世 (yì shēng yí shì), which means "All life long".

There are other things to talk about related to numbers, which can be covered in more advanced lessons.

Chapter 4: How to be polite when speaking Chinese?

Native Chinese speakers have a paragraph summarizing the key point to be polite. In this chapter, our main objective is to learn about this paragraph. If you can bear this paragraph in mind and use it accordingly when speaking Chinese, your listeners will surely consider you to be a very polite person. You may keep in mind that you don't really need to use these expressions with someone close to you as they are far too formal. Here is the paragraph.

请人帮忙说劳驾，请给方便说借光。

麻烦别人说打扰，不知适宜用冒昧。

求人解答用请问，请人指点用赐教。

赞人见解用高见，自己意见用拙见。

看望别人用拜访，宾客来到用光临。

陪伴朋友用奉陪，中途先走用失陪。

等候客人用恭候，迎接表歉用失迎。

别人离开用再见，请人不送用留步。

欢迎顾客称光顾，答人问候用托福。

问人年龄用贵庚，老人年龄用高寿。

读人文章用拜读,请人改文用斧正。

对方字画为墨宝,自己字画用拙笔。

邀请别人用屈驾,招待不周说怠慢。

请人收礼用笑纳,辞谢馈赠用心领。

问人姓氏用贵姓,回答询问用免贵。

表演技能用献丑,别人赞扬说过奖。

向人祝贺道恭喜,答人道贺用同喜。

请人担职用屈就,暂时充任说承乏。

对方亲眷多带令,称呼己方常带家。

qǐng rén bāng máng shuō láo jià, qǐng gěi fāng biàn shuō jiè guāng

má fán bié rén shuō dǎ rǎo, bù zhī shì yí yòng mào mèi

qiú rén jiě dá yòng qǐng wèn, qǐng rén zhǐ diǎn yòng cì jiào

zàn rén jiàn jiě yòng gāo jiàn, zì jǐ yì jiàn yòng zhuō jiàn

kàn wàng bié rén yòng bài fǎng, bīn kè lái dào yòng guāng lín

péi bàn péng yǒu yòng fèng péi, zhōng tú xiān zǒu yòng shī péi

děng hòu kè rén yòng gōng hòu, yíng jiē biǎo qiàn yòng shī yíng

bié rén lí kāi yòng zài jiàn, qǐng rén bú sòng yòng liú bù

huān yíng gù kè chēng guāng gù, dá rén wèn hòu yòng tuō fú

wèn rén nián líng yòng guì gēng, lǎo rén nián líng yòng gāo shòu

dú rén wén zhāng yòng bài dú, qǐng rén gǎi wén yòng fǔ zhèng

duì fāng zì huà wéi mò bǎo, zì jǐ zì huà yòng zhuō bǐ

yāo qǐng bié rén yòng qū jià, zhāo dài bùzhōu shuō dài màn

qǐng rén shōu lǐ yòng xiào nà, cí xiè kuì zèng yòng xīn lǐng

wèn rén xìng shì yòng guì xìng, huí dá xún wèn yòng miǎn guì biǎo yǎn jì néng yòng xiàn chǒu, bié rén zàn yáng shuō guò jiǎng

xiàng rén zhù hè dào gōng xǐ, dá rén dào hè yòng tóng xǐ

qǐng rén dān zhí yòng qū jiù, zàn shí chōng rèn shuō chéng fá

duì fāng qīn juàn duō dài lìng, chēng hū jǐ fāng cháng dài jiā

Don't panic! We will analyze this paragraph sentence by sentence. After we finish this chapter, you will see how easy it is to remember the ways to express yourself politely.

请人帮忙说劳驾，请给方便说借光（qǐng rén bāng máng shuō láo jià, qǐng gěi fāng biàn shuō jiè guāng）。

When asking for a favor, remember to use 劳驾（láo jià）which means please. For example:

劳驾帮我拿一下（láo jià bāng wǒ náyí xià）。

Please help me hold this.

When you want to move some where but someone is blocking your way, remember to say 借光（jiè guāng）which means excuse me. For example:

借光，我过去（jiè guāng, wǒ guò qù）。

Excuse me, please let me pass.

麻烦别人说打扰，不知适宜用冒昧（má fán bié rén shuō dǎ rǎo, bù zhī shì yí yòng mào mèi）。

When you have some questions to ask a stranger, you can say 打扰了（dǎ rǎo le）which means sorry to bother you. If you are not sure whether it is OK or when it is appropriate to ask the question, you can use 冒昧（mào mèi）to start the sentence. For example:

打扰一下，请问机场在哪（dǎ rǎo yí xià, qǐng wèn jī chǎng zài nǎ）？

Sorry to bother you, could you please show me the way to the airport?

冒昧问一句，我能走了吗（mào mèi wèn yí jù, wǒ néng zǒu le ma）？

Excuse me, when can I leave? **求人解答用**请问，请人指点用赐教（qiú rén jiě dá yòng qǐng wèn, qǐng rén zhǐ diǎn yòng cì jiào）。

When asking questions, remember to use "请问"（qǐng wèn）. When you need someone to help you to solve a problem, use 赐教（cì jiào）to show modesty. For example:

请问你叫什么名字（qǐng wèn nǐ jiào shénme míng zì）？

May I have your name please?

这道题我实在想不出来，不知您能否赐教（zhè dào tí wǒ shí zài xiǎng bù chū lái, bù zhī nín néng fǒu cì jiào）？

I really can't solve this problem, could you please help me out?

赞人见解用高见，自己意见用拙见（zàn rén jiàn jiě yòng gāo jiàn, zì jǐ yì jiàn yòng zhuō jiàn）。

When complimenting someone's opinions, use 高见（gāo jiàn）. While mentioning your own opinions, use 拙见（zhuō jià）. For example:

您的这番高见让我获益匪浅（nín de zhè fān gāo jiàn ràng wǒ huò yì fěi qiǎn）。

Your wonderful opinion has benefited me a lot.

小小拙见，让您见笑了（xiǎo xiǎo zhuō jiàn, ràng nín jiàn xiào le）。

Please pardon me with my limited thoughts.

看望别人用拜访，宾客来到用光临（kàn wàng bié rén yòng bài fǎng, bīn kè lái dào yòng guāng lín）。

When visiting a client, supervisor, or a senior, use 拜访（bài fǎng）. When you are welcoming visitors, use 光临（guāng lín). For example:

有时间我想拜访一下你的父母（yǒu shí jiān wǒ xiǎng bài fǎng yíxià nǐ de fù mǔ）。

I would like to visit your parents when I have time.

非常感谢您的光临（fēi cháng gǎn xiè nín de guāng lín）。

Thank you for visiting us.

陪伴朋友用奉陪，中途先走用失陪（péi bàn péng yǒu yòng fèng péi, zhōng tú xiān zǒu yòng shī péi）。

When accompanying friends, you can use 奉陪（fèng péi）. If you need to leave at the middle of an event/activity, don't forget to use 失陪（shī péi). For example:

大家都是朋友，那我就奉陪到底了（dà jiā dōu shì péng yǒu, nà wǒ jiù fèng péi dào dǐ le）。

We're all friends, so I'll be withyou to the end.

我有点急事需要处理，失陪了（wǒ yǒu diǎn jí shì xū yào chù lǐ, shī péi le）。

I'm sorry for leavng early because of something urgent.等候客人用恭候，迎接表歉用失迎（děng hòu kè rén yòng gōng hòu, yíng jiē biǎo qiàn yòng shī yíng）。

When waiting for esteemed guests to arrive, use 恭候（gōng hòu）. If you've missed your guests or they arrived before you, you can use 失迎（shī yíng). For example:

我们会在此恭候您的大驾（wǒ men huì zài cǐ gōng hòu nín de dà jià）。

We're honored to await your arrival.

不好意思，失迎了（bù hǎo yì sī, shī yíng le）。

I'm really sorry for not welcoming you earlier.

别人离开用再见，请人不送用留步（bié rén lí kāi yòng zài jiàn, qǐng rén bú sòng yòng liú bù）。

When parting with someone, don't forget to say 再见（zài jiàn）. If someone insists on accompanying you to the last minute, you can say 留步（liú bù）.

非常感谢您的热情招待，请留步（fēi cháng gǎn xiè nín de rè qíng zhāo dài, qǐng liú bù）。

Thank you very much for your warm hospitality; you don't need to see me out.

欢迎顾客称光顾，答人问候用托福（huān yíng gù kè chēng guāng gù, dá rén wèn hòu yòng tuō fú）。

When expressing your gratitude to your visitors, you can use 光顾（guāng gù）. When answering someone's questions related to your current statusor situation, you can use 托福（tuō fú). For example:

非常感谢您的光顾（fēi cháng gǎn xiè nín de guāng gù）。

Thank you very much for visiting us.

最近怎么样？——托您的福，一切安好（zuì jìn zěn me yàng？——tuō nín de fú, yí qiè ān hǎo）。

How are you lately?——Everything's fine, thank you for asking.

问人年龄用贵庚，老人年龄用高寿（wèn rén nián líng yòng guì gēng, lǎo rén nián líng yòng gāo shòu）。

When asking someone's age, you can use the word 贵庚（guì gēng）, but don't use this word when asking kids. For a senior, you should use the word 高寿（gāo shòu）.

In traditional Chinese culture, age is not considered to be private. It is a topic often brought up in social occasions. Nevertheless, different ways are employed to ask about the age of different people. For kids younger than ten, people ask "你今年几岁了?"（nǐ jīn nián jǐ suì le） For a young person or someone of one's own age, one may ask "你今年多大了?"（nǐ jīn nián duō dà le） or the polite way, "您贵庚（nín guì gēng）?". For an elder person, however, one should use "您高寿（nín gāo shòu）?" to show respect.

读人文章用拜读，请人改文用斧正（dú rén wén zhāng yòng bài dú, qǐng rén gǎi wén yòng fǔ zhèng）。

When reading someone's paperwork, use the word 拜读（bài dú）, when you need someone to proofread your paperwork, use the word 斧正（fǔ zhèng）. For example:

听说您的论文出版了，能否拜读一下（tīng shuō nín de lùn wén chū bǎn le, néng fǒu bài dú yī xià）？

I heard that your essay has been published; could I read it?

我的稿子写完了，请斧正（wǒ de gǎo zǐ xiě wán le, qǐng fǔ zhèng）。

I've finished writing my paper; please proofread it.

对方字画为墨宝，自己字画用拙笔（duì fāng zì huà wéi mò bǎo, zì jǐ zì huà yòng zhuō bǐ）。

If you want to compliment someone's painting, use the word 墨宝（mò bǎo）. If you paint, and you would like someone to look at it, use the word 拙笔（zhuō bǐ）. For example:

让我来欣赏一下您的墨宝（ràng wǒ lái xīn shǎng yī xià nín de mò bǎo）。

Please allow me to enjoy your masterpiece.

我这里也有一些拙笔，请您过目（wǒ zhè lǐ yě yǒu yī xiē zhuō bǐ, qǐng nín guò mù）。

I have here some of my paintings; please take a look.

邀请别人用屈驾，招待不周说怠慢（yāo qǐng bié rén yòng qū jià, zhāo dài bú zhōu shuō dài màn）。

If you want to invite someone to go with you, remember to use the word 屈驾（qū jià）. If you're treating your guests, you can use the word 怠慢（dài màn). For example:

请问您能屈驾跟我走一趟吗（qǐng wèn nín néng qū jià gēn wǒ zǒu yī tàng ma）？

Are you able to travel with me?

招待不周，多有怠慢，请见谅（zhāo dài bú zhōu, duō yǒu dài màn, qǐng jiàn liàng）。

Please forgive me for the oversight.

请人收礼用笑纳，辞谢馈赠用心领（qǐng rén shōu lǐ yòng xiào nà, cí xiè kuì zèng yòng xīn lǐng）。

When you are giving gift to someone, you can use 笑纳（xiào nà）. When refusing someone's gift, you can say 心领（xīn lǐng）. For example:

小小薄礼，请笑纳（xiǎo xiǎo báo lǐ, qǐng xiào nà）。

Please accept this small gift.

您的礼物我心领了（nín de lǐ wù wǒ xīn lǐng le）。

Thank you for the gift. I must reject, but I've taken it to heart.

问人姓氏用贵姓，回答询问用免贵（wèn rén xìng shì yòng guì xìng, huí dá xún wèn yòng miǎn guì）。

When asking for someone's surname, use the word 贵姓（guì xìng）. To answer the question, start the sentence with 免贵（miǎn guì）. We'll analyze these in the next chapter.

表演技能用献丑，别人赞扬说过奖（biǎo yǎn jì néng yòng xiàn chǒu, bié rén zàn yáng shuō guò jiǎng）。

When you want to put on a performance, like singing or dancing, you can use 献丑（xiàn chǒu）. If the audience likes your show and compliments you, you can use 过奖（guò jiǎng）to respond. For example:

既然大家盛情难却，那我就献丑唱上一段（jì rán dà jiā shèng qíng nán què, nà wǒ jiù xiàn chǒu chàng shàng yí duàn）。

Thank you for your warm invitation. I'll embarrass myself and sing a song.

您唱得真好！——您过奖了（nín chàng dé zhēn hǎo!——nín guò jiǎng le）。

You sing really well!——You're far too kind.

向人祝贺道恭喜，答人道贺用同喜（xiàng rén zhù hè dào gōng xǐ, dá rén dào hè yòng tóng xǐ）。

When something good happens to someone, and you are happy for him, you can use 恭喜（gōng xǐ）. As a response to 恭喜（gōng xǐ）, you can use 同喜（tóng xǐ）.

我成功了（wǒ chéng gōng le）！——真是恭喜你（zhēn shì gōng xǐ nǐ le）了。——同喜同喜（tóng xǐ tóng xǐ）！

I've succeeded!——Congratulations!——Thank you.

请人担职用屈就，暂时充任说承乏（qǐng rén dān zhí yòng qū jiù, zàn shí chōng rèn shuō chéng fá）。

If you are trying to offer an important corporate position to someone, you can use the phrase 屈就（qū jiù）. On the contrary, if someone is offering a position to you, you should use the word 承乏（chéng fá）.

不知您能否屈就我司总经理一职（bú zhī nín néng fǒu qū jiù wǒ sī zǒng jīng lǐ yī zhí）？

Would you mind accepting the offer of being the general manager of our company?

既然如此，我只好承乏其位了（jì rán rú cǐ, wǒ zhǐ hǎo chéng fá qí wèi le）。

I'll have to take the job if you insist, but if you find someone better, please replace me.

对方亲眷多带令，称呼己方常带家（duì fāng qīn juàn duō dài lìng, chēng hū jǐ fāng cháng dài jiā）。

Just take some examples here:

令尊（lìng zūn）, your father

令堂（lìng táng）, your mother

令爱（lìng ài）, your daughter

令郎（lìng láng）, your son

家父（jiā fù）, my father

家母（jiā mǔ）, my mother

All these mentioned are pronouns, very hard pronouns. So just try to keep them in mind for some additional understnading. We'll have detailed discussions in our advanced books.

All in all, due to cultural differences, many of the polite expressions may be strange for an English speaker. You may be able to tell when reading the translation. Please remember here, many translations are just literally translated from Chinese so as to help your understanding.

Chapter 5: Greeting and Introduction

We'll introduce you a sample paragraph here, then we'll discuss some of the most commonly used sentences and practice speaking them one by one. If you can remember these, you should be able to form your own sentences.

大家早上好，**我叫**张阳，来自中国，很高兴认识大家。五年前，我大学毕业并取得学士学位，我的专业是中国文学。我当时的梦想是成为一名记者，因此毕业后，我到处寻找工作，在不同的报社实习。现在我是一个网络小说作者，我很喜欢我现在的工作，**因**为我有时间可以到处旅行。我去过很多国家，比如日本、韩国、美国和澳大利亚。每个国家都有各自的特色，我特别喜欢美国的现代和繁华。在独自旅行的时候，我结识了很多朋友。因为资金有限，我在每个国家呆的时间都不会太长，虽然停留不了多久，但我每天都很高兴。哦，对了，我还没有结婚，也没有孩子。

我出生于1992年3月1日，**今年**27岁。我没有兄弟姐妹，爸爸妈妈就只有我一个孩子，我现在自己住在北京的公寓里。我的爸爸是一名医生，妈妈是一名中学教师，他们住在上海。我的父母养了一条可爱的小狗，名字叫**豆豆**，每次回家，晚上我都会带它去**公园散步**。**上海有我很多小**时候的朋友，他们有的已经结婚生子，有的还在继续上学。我们有时会约好见个面，一同谈谈学习、工作和生活中的事。总之，我对现在很满意。感谢你来听我的故事，再见。

dà jiā zǎo shàng hǎo, wǒ jiào zhāng yáng, lái zì zhōng guó, hěn gāo xìng rèn shí dà jiā. wǔ nián qián, wǒ dà xué bì yè bìng qǔ dé xué shì xué wèi, wǒ de zhuān yè shì zhōng guó wén xué. wǒ dāng shí de mèng xiǎng shì chéng wéi yìmíng jì zhě, yīn cǐ bì yè hòu, wǒ dào chù xún zhǎo gōng zuò, zài bú tóng de bào shè shí xí. xiàn zài wǒ shìyígè wǎng luò xiǎo shuō zuò zhě, wǒ hěn xǐ huān wǒ xiàn zài de gōng zuò, yīn wéi wǒ yǒu shí jiān kě yǐ dào chù lǚxíng. wǒ qù guò hěn duō guó jiā, bǐ rú rì běn, hán guó, měi guó hé ào dà lì yà. měi gè guó jiā dōu yǒu gè zì de tè sè, wǒ tè bié xǐ huān měi guó de xiàn dài hé fán huá. zài dú zì lǚxíngde shí hòu, wǒ jié shí le hěn duō péng yǒu. yīn wéi zī jīn yǒu xiàn, wǒ zài měi gè guó jiā dāi de shí jiān dōu bú huì tàicháng, suī rán tíng liú bùliǎo duō jiǔ, dàn wǒ měi tiān dōu hěn gāo xìng. o, duì le, wǒ hái méi yǒu jié hūn, yě méi yǒu háizi.

wǒ chū shēng yú yī jiǔ jiǔ èr nián sān yuè yī rì, jīn nián èr shí qī suì. wǒ méi yǒu xiōng dì jiě mèi, bà ba mā ma jiùzhǐyǒu wǒyígè hái zi, wǒ xiàn zài zì jǐ zhù zài běi jīng de gōng yù lǐ. wǒ de bà ba shìyìmíng yī shēng, mā ma shìyìmíng zhōng xué jiào shī, tā men zhù zài shàng hǎi. wǒ de fù mǔ yǎng le yìtiáo kě ài de xiǎo gǒu, míng zì jiào dòudou, měi cì huí jiā, wǎn shàng wǒ dōu huì dài tā qù gōng yuán sàn bù. shàng hǎi yǒu wǒ hěn duō xiǎo shí hòu de péng yǒu, tā men yǒu de yǐ jīng jié hūn shēng zǐ, yǒu de hái zài jì xù shàng xué. wǒ men yǒu shí huì yuē hǎo jiàn gè miàn, yìtóng tán tán xué xí, gōng zuò hé shēng huó zhōng de shì. zǒng zhī, wǒ duì xiàn zài hěn mǎn yì. xièxieni lái tīng wǒ de gù shì, zài jiàn.

Now, let's analyze this paragraph sentence by sentence.

大家早上好,**我叫**张阳,来自中国,很高兴认识大家。(dà jiā zǎo shàng hǎo, wǒ jiào zhāng yáng, lái zì zhōng guó, hěn gāo xìng rèn shí dà jiā)。

Good morning, everyone. My name is Zhang Yang. I'm from China; nice to meet you all.

In most places, you will get a warm and friendly response to your enthusiasm in speaking Chinese. A conversation can be struck and acquaintances made with just a few words.

The most often used greeting, appropriate for all occasions, is 你好 (nǐ hǎo). That said, when Chinese people meet, various amenities and civilities are exchanged. For instance:

你好!好久不见,最近好吗(nǐ hǎo! hǎo jiǔ bú jiàn, zuì jìn hǎo ma)?

How are you? We haven't seen each other for such a long time. How are you lately? 工作怎么样?忙吗(gōng zuò zěn me yàng? máng ma)?

How's your work? Have you been busy?

身体好吗?家里人都好吧(shēn tǐ hǎo ma? jiā lǐ rén dōu hǎo ba)?

Are you well? Is your family well?

你去哪儿(nǐ qù nǎ ér)?

Where are you going?

吃了吗(chī le ma)?

Have you eaten yet?

孩子学习怎么样(hái zi xué xí zěn me yàng)?

How are the children doing in their studies?

听说你前些天去外地了,什么时候回来的(tīng shuō nǐ qián xiē tiān qù wài dì le, shén me shí hòu huí lái de)?

I heard that you went away a few days ago. When did you get back?

你好像瘦了（nǐ hǎo xiàng shòu le）?

You seem to be losing weight.

几天不见，你更漂亮了（jǐ tiān bú jiàn, nǐ gèng piàoliàng le）!

I haven't seen you for a few days; you've become prettier!

冷吗? 你穿的太少了，小心别感冒（lěng ma? nǐ chuān de tài shǎo le, xiǎo xīn bié gǎn mào）!

Aren't you cold? You're wearing so little, be careful not to catch a cold!

这件衣服挺漂亮的，是新买的（zhè jiàn yī fú tǐng piàoliàng de, shì xīn mǎi de）?

This is a beautiful dress; did you just buy it?

The other party may give a truthful and factual answer or just a brief answer like 还可以（hái kě yǐ, passable）, 挺好的（tǐng hǎo de, quite well）, 不太忙（bú tài máng, not very busy）, 我出去了一趟（wǒ chū qù le yítàng, I went away）, 吃了（chī le, I had dinner）. Thesequestions indicate that the person asking them is concerned about you or interested in you. There's no reason to feel uncomfortable or upset since they're just amenities.

When coming across someone, the Chinese don't often say 你好（nǐ hǎo, how are you）or 早上好（zǎo shàng hǎo, good morning）. They are used to asking questions about what you are doing or what you're about to do in accordance with the time or situation. For instance: 上课去呀（shàng kè qù ya, going to class?）? 出去呀（chū qù ya, going out?）? 回来啦（huí láila, you're back?）? 洗衣服呢（xǐ yī fú ne, doing laundry?）? 吃饭呢（chī fàn ne, eating?）?, Etc.

When parting from each other, some common civilities include but are limited to:

我还有点儿别的事，改天咱们好好儿聊聊（wǒ hái yǒu diǎn ér bié de shì, gǎi tiān zán men hǎo hǎo ér liáoliao）。

I have something else to attend to, so let's have a chat some other time.

有空儿来家里坐坐（yǒu kōng ér lái jiā lǐ zuòzuo）。

Come and visit us when you have time.

But this may just be polite convention, and may not necessarily be an invitation. Only when the date and time is given is it meant as an invitation.

"我叫（wǒ jiào）……" is the answer to "你叫什么名字（nǐ jiào shénme míngzi）?"——What is your name?

你叫什么名字（nǐ jiào shénme míng zi）is used to ask someone for his or her full name. 您（nín）is a more polite form of 你（nǐ）. It is usually used for seniors or people of an older generation or a higher rank. It can also be used for people of the same age in order to sound more formal and polite. The answer can also be 我是（wǒ shì）…, usually giving both the surname and the first name.

We can use a respectful and polite way of asking for the surname of someone you have just met for the first time: 您贵姓（nín guì xìng）? This person would reply with "免贵姓（miǎn guì xìng）……"

A Chinese name starts with the family name and ends with the given name. There are over 5,000 Chinese family names, among which more than 200 are commonly seen. 张（zhāng），王（wáng），李（lǐ），and 赵（zhào）are the most common ones. Such family names that have only one character are known as single-character surnames. Most Chinese people have a single-character surname. There are surnames with two or more characters also, which are called compound-character surnames, such as 欧阳 (ōu yáng), 上官 (shàng guān), and 诸葛 (zhū gě). Try to find your own Chinese name!

A person can be addressed with his/her family name followed by his/her job or profession. For instance, 张阳 (zhāng yáng) is a teacher, so we can call her 张老师 (zhāng lǎo shī) - literally, it means Teacher Zhang.

"来自中国 (lái zì zhōng guó)" is the answer to "你是哪国人 (nǐ shì nǎ guó rén)?" ——Where are you from?

It is used to inquire the nationality of someone having the same meaning with "你从哪儿来 (nǐ cóng nǎ ér lái)?"

You can also reply by saying "我是从……来的 (wǒ shì cóng ……lái de)" This structure is used to explain the place where you come from.

我很高兴认识你/您 (wǒ hěn gāo xìng rèn shi nǐ /nín)。

It's nice to meet you.

It is used when meeting someone for the first time. The answer is "我也是 (wǒ yě shì)" which means "me, too". If it's not the first time, you need to say "我很高兴见到你/您 (wǒ hěn gāo xìng jiàn dào nǐ /nín)" which means "it's good to see you". The answer can be the same.

五年前，我大学毕业并取得学士学位，我的专业是中国文学 (wǔ nián qián, wǒ dà xué bì yè bìng qǔ dé xué shì xué wèi, wǒ de zhuān yè shì zhōng guó wén xué)。

Five years ago, I graduated from university with a bachelor's degree. My major was Chinese Literature.

With this sentence you can talk about your education, your major, and even your campus life. Questions you may hear Chinese people ask include:

你是大学生吗（nǐ shì dà xué shēng ma）？

Are you a university student?

大几了（dà jǐ le）？

What grade?

什么专业（shén me zhuān yè）？

What is your major?

我当时的梦想是成为一名记者，因此毕业后，我到处寻找工作，在不同的报社实习（wǒ dāng shí de mèng xiǎng shì chéng wéi yì míng jì zhě, yīn cǐ bì yè hòu, wǒ dào chù xún zhǎo gōng zuò, zài bú tóng de bào shè shí xí）。

My dream by then was to be a journalist. Therefore, after graduation, I looked for jobs everywhere, and did internship at many different newspaper offices.

This can be used to talk about your past experiences. Because verbs in Chinese do not need to change according to the tense, talking about the past, present, or future has no difference for the verbs. You need only add different adverbials of time.

现在我是一个网络小说作者，我很喜欢我现在的工作，因为我有时间可以到处旅行（xiàn zài wǒ shìyígè wǎng luò xiǎo shuō zuò zhě, wǒ hěn xǐ huān wǒ xiàn zài de gōng zuò, yīn wéi wǒ yǒu shí jiān kě yǐ dào chù lǚxíng）。

I'm now making a living by writing novelsonline. I love what I am doing right now because I have plenty of time to travel all over the world.

This can be used to introduce your current situation.

我去过很多国家，比如日本、韩国、美国和澳大利亚 (wǒ qù guò hěn duō guó jiā, bǐ rú rì běn, hán guó, měi guó hé ào dà lì yà) 。

I've been to many different countries, such as Japan, South Korea, America, and Australia.

Each country has their Chinese name, as well as major cities, famous places, beautiful sights, cuisine, celebrities, movies, etc. You have to remember these proper nouns every time you learn them. A sidenote--Hong Kong and Taiwan may use different versions of these proper nouns. Don't worry about it too much for now. Rome was not built in a day.

每个国家都有各自的特色，我特别喜欢美国的现代和繁华
(měi gè guó jiā dōu yǒu gè zì de tè sè, wǒ tè bié xǐ huān měi guó de xiàn dài hé fán huá) 。

Every country has its own characteristics. I especially like the prosperous and moderness of America.

"我喜欢（wǒ xǐ huān）……" is used to express someone's affirmation towards something, the negationis "我不喜欢（wǒ bù xǐ huān）……"

By changing the pronoun or adding the particle, we can form many different sentences, for example:

你喜欢美国的什么呢（nǐ xǐ huān měi guó de shénme ne）?

What do you like about America?

她应该喜欢唱歌吧（tā yīng gāi xǐ huān chàng gē ba）?

She likes to sing, doesn't she?

在独自旅行的时候，我结识了很多朋友 (zài dú zì lǚxíngde shí hòu, wǒ jié shí le hěn duō péng yǒu) 。

While travelling alone, I met and became friends with many different people.

Here, you can add your own travel stories to make your speech more interesting.

因为资金有限，我在每个国家呆的时间都不会太长，虽然停留不了多久，但我每天都很高兴（yīn wéi zī jīn yǒu xiàn, wǒ zài měi gè guó jiā dāi de shí jiān dōu bú huì tàicháng, suī rán tíng liú bùliǎoduō jiǔ, dàn wǒ měi tiān dōu hěn gāo xìng）。

Because of my limited budget, I couldn't stay long in the countries I travelled to. Though I couldn't stay for a long time, I felt happy every day when I was there.

When someone asks you "how did you enjoy your trip?" you can also answer like so.

哦，对了，我还没有结婚，也没有孩子（o, duì le, wǒ hái méi yǒu jié hūn, yě méi yǒu hái zi）。

Oh right, I still haven't got married, and I don't have anychild.

结婚（jié hūn）here, 结（jié）is a verb, 婚（hūn）is marriage,combined together, 结婚（jié hūn）means to get married.. Similar, 离婚（lí hūn），to get divorced；订婚（dìng hūn），to get engaged.

我出生于1992年3月1日，今年27岁（wǒ chū shēng yú yī jiǔ jiǔ èr nián sān yuè yī rì, jīn nián èr shí qī suì）。I was born in Mar. 1, 1992. I'm 27 years old.

Compared with English, Chinese people use the time order of year-month-day-hour-minute-second. Try to get out of the standard English format when speaking Chinese.

As we mentioned earlier, in traditional Chinese culture, age is not considered private. It is a topic often brought up in social occasions, so don't feel uncomfortable when receiving questions asking about your age. In addition, when seniors meet you again after a long time, they may say "你胖了（nǐ pàng le）" which literally means "you've gotten fat", but actually they just mean "you've been well" or "you are in good health". No needed to be offended.

我没有兄弟姐妹，爸爸妈妈就只有我一个孩子，我现在自己住在北京的公寓里（wǒ méi yǒu xiōng dì jiě mèi, bàbamābajiùzhǐyǒu wǒyígè hái zi, wǒ xiàn zài zì jǐ zhù zài běi jīng de gōng yù lǐ）。

I have no brothers or sisters. I'm my parents' only child. I live in an apartment in Beijing by myself.

In China, people often ask about their friends' parents or children during conversations to show respect and concern, and people asked are normally pleased about this. Therefore, talking about family is one of the most important aspects in a conversation. In Chinese, the pronouns 哥哥/弟弟/姐姐/妹妹（gē ge/ dì di/ jiě jie/ mèi mei）equate to older / younger brother and older / younger sister in English. No adjective is needed to modify the pronoun.

Because of the one-child policy, most Chinese families have been single-child households. Citizens that lived in the city were allowed to give birth to one child while citizens that lived in the countryside were allowed to give birth to a second only if the first was a girl. If people broke the rule, they had to pay for a huge penalty. Now, however, the Chinese government allows all the citizens to give birth to two children.

我的爸爸是一名医生，妈妈是一名中学教师，他们住在上海（wǒ de bàbashìyìmíng yī shēng, māmashìyìmíng zhōng xué jiào shī, tā men zhù zài shàng hǎi）。

My father is a doctor and my mother is a middle school teacher; they live in Shanghai now.

When talking about occupation, just remember the sentence structure: personal pronoun + 是（shì）+ 一位/一名（yí wèi/ yì míng）+ occupation. For the places the person is working: personal pronoun + work in + places/ companies. Sometimes, the latter can be used to answer the question of occupation. For example:

你爸爸做什么工作（nǐ bà bà zuòshén me gōng zuò）？——他是一名翻译（tā shìyì míng fān yì）。

What is your father's job?——He's a translator.

她老公做什么工作（tā lǎo gōng zuòshén me gōng zuò）？——她老公在一家研究所工作（tā lǎo gōng zài yì jiā yán jiū suǒ gōng zuò）。

What is her husband's job?——Her husband works in a research institute.

我的父母养了一条可爱的小狗，名字叫豆豆，每次回家，晚上我都会带它去公园散步（wǒ de fù mǔ yǎng le yì tiáo kě ài de xiǎo gǒu, míng zì jiào dòudou, měi cì huí jiā, wǎn shàng wǒ dōu huì dài tā qù gōng yuán sàn bù）。

My parents have a very lovely dog called Doudou; I walk it through the park every time I go home.

In China, cats and dogs are as popular as they are in many other countries. When naming pets, Chinese people often use some cute names like they use tochildren. Some common pet names are 贝贝（bèibei），**豆豆**（dòudou），欢欢（huānhuan），乐乐（lè le），小花（xiǎo huā），喵喵（miāomiao），etc. So when you are trying to choose a Chinese name, please avoid these names. Just imagine Chinese people choosing their English name as Honey, Sweety, Hero, April, Precious...you can't helplaughing, right? So it's best to avoid these names.

上海有我很多小时候的朋友，他们有的已经结婚生子，有的还在继续上学（shàng hǎi yǒu wǒ hěn duō xiǎo shí hòu de péng

yǒu, tā men yǒu de yǐ jīng jié hūn shēng zǐ, yǒu de hái zài jì xù shàng xué)。

I have many friends in Shanghai whom I've known since a young age. Some of them have already gotten married and even had kids; some of them are still students.

In Chinese, 有的（yǒu de）……有的（yǒu de）……is a really common structure. This structure indicates a parallel relationship. We can use it in many other situations as well. For example:

他们有的人睡觉，有的人看书（tā men yǒu de rén shuì jiào，yǒu de rén kàn shū）。

Some of them are sleeping while some of them are reading a book.

公园里有的人散步，有的人跳舞（gōng yuán lǐ yǒu de rén sàn bù，yǒu de rén tiào wǔ）。

There are many people in the park; some of them are walking while some of them are dancing.

我们有时会约好见个面，一同谈谈学习、工作和生活中的事（wǒ men yǒu shí huì yuē hǎo jiàn gè miàn, yì tóng tán tan xué xí, gōng zuò hé shēng huó zhōng de shì）。

Sometimes, we'll pick a time and get together to talk about things thosehappened during studies, work, or daily life.

Sometimes among friends, especially among those who have the same aspirations and interests, a periodic talk is held and it's somewhat of an academic discussion. A periodic talk is usually prearranged and requires some preparations. People would talk about a certain aspect of work or study so as to exchange thoughts and share common ideas. So if you really want to start this part of the conversation, you need to learn a lot and of course, keep learning. We will provide more topics in our advanced books.

总之，我对现在很满意（zǒng zhī, wǒ duì xiàn zài hěn mǎn yì）。

All in all, I'm very satisfied with my current situation.

When someone asks you "are you happy?" or questions like this, you can then introduce your current situation and come up with your conclusion in the end by using this sentence. Some examples of positive situations are:

我现在很快乐（wǒ xiàn zài hěn kuài lè）。

I'm pretty happy now.

我很享受现在的生活（wǒ hěn xiǎng shòu xiàn zài de shēng huó）。

I'm enjoying my life right now.

For negative conclusions, expect putting 不（bù）to the proper positions of the sentences, you can use the word like 难过/失落/寂寞（nán guò / shī luò / jì mò）instead of 满意/快乐/享受（mǎn yì/ kuài lè/ xiǎng shòu）。For example:

我现在很寂寞（wǒ xiàn zài hěn jì mò）。

I'm really lonely right now.

现在的生活让我很失落（xiàn zài de shēng huó ràng wǒ hěn shī luò）。

I feel very sorry for myself.

谢谢你来听我的故事，再见（xièxie nǐ lái tīng wǒ de gù shì, zài jiàn）。

Thank you for listening to my story. Goodbye.

The respond to 谢谢（xièxie）is 不谢/不用谢/不客气（bú xiè/ bú yòng xiè/ bú kè qì） which means "you're welcome", or "my pleasure".

As in English, there are many ways in Chinese to express "goodbye" or "see you later". When parting with someone, you may also include the time or location at which you will again see the other party, for example:

明天见（míng tiān jiàn）。

See you tomorrow.

一会儿见（yí huì ér jiàn）。

See you soon.

下周见（xià zhōu jiàn）。

See you next week.

门口见（mén kǒu jiàn）。

See you at the gate.

You can also use 一路平安/一路顺风（yí lù píng ān /yí lù shùn fēng） to say goodbye or to wish someone a safe journey.

Last but not least, asking about other people's stories is as interesting as telling them your own stories. In order to start and continue an exchange of stories, get to learn the questions listed. We're expected to come up with questions as well as giving responses.

Chapter 6: Daily Life and Social Activity

After learning some things related to grammar, we can finally go back to the practicing. Because this book is limited in length, we will only focus on different sentences in this chapter. For more explanations and language points, please refer to our advanced books.

In a Restaurant

你想吃什么（nǐ xiǎng chī shén me）？

What do you want to eat?

有沙拉吗（yǒu shā lā ma）？

Is there any salad?

这里面是什么（zhè lǐ miàn shì shén me）？

What's in this dish?

我要这个（wǒ yào zhè gè）。

I want this.

给我两碗米饭（gěi wǒ liǎng wǎn mǐ fàn）。

Two bowls of rice, please.

米饭和菜一起上（mǐ fàn hé cài yì qǐ shàng）。

Please bring the rice and dish together.

还要些什么（hái yào xiē shén me）？

What else do you want?

就要这些（jiù yào zhè xiē）。

These will be enough.

不要了（bú yào le）。

Nothing else.

我们不吃螃蟹（wǒ men bù chī páng xiè）。

We don't like to eat crab.

再来一瓶果汁（zài lái yì píng guǒ zhī）。

A cup of juice, please.

我要买单（wǒ yào mǎi dān）。

I'll pay the bill.

我们要发票和收据（wǒ men yào fā piào hé shōu jù）。

Wewant the receipt and invoice.

可以打包吗（kě yǐ dǎ bāo ma）？

Can I pack the remaining food?

In a Shop

您要买什么（nín yào mǎi shén me）？

What do you want to buy?

我看看（wǒ kànkan）。

Let me see.

这个多少钱（zhè gè duō shǎo qián）？

How much is this?

打折吗（dǎ zhé ma）？

Can I get a discount?

太贵了（tài guì le）。

(That's) too expensive.

能便宜一点吗（néng pián yiyìdiǎn ma）？

Can you make it a little cheaper?

还有别的颜色吗（hái yǒu bié de yán sè ma）？

Do you have another color?

有没有更好的（yǒu méi yǒu gèng hǎo de）？

Do you havea better one?

能换一个吗（néng huàn yí gè ma）？

Can you show me another one?

我喜欢这条裤子（wǒ xǐ huān zhè tiáo kùzi）。

I like these pants.

能试一试吗（néng shìyí shì ma）？

Can I try them on?

In a Taxi

你要去哪里（nǐ yào qù nǎ lǐ）？

Where are you going?

去超市（qù chāo shì）。

I'm going to the supermarket.

请开一下后备箱（qǐng kāi yí xià hòu bèi xiāng）。

Please open the trunk.

你知道怎么去超市吗（nǐ zhī dào zěn me qù chāo shì ma）？

Do you know how to get to the supermarket?

请快一点（qǐng kuài yì diǎn）。

Please hurry up.

请不要开太快（qǐng bú yào kāi tài kuài）。

Please don't drive too fast.

大概要多少时间（dà gài yào duō shǎo shí jiān）？

How long do you need to go there?

你能停一下吗（nǐ néng tíng yíxià ma）？

Can you stop for a minute?

你能等我十分钟吗（nǐ néng děng wǒ shí fèn zhōng ma）？

Can you wait for me for like ten minutes?

你有零钱吗（nǐ yǒu líng qián ma）？

Do you have change?

去机场多少钱（qù jī chǎng duō shǎo qián）？

How much from here to the airport?

On the Road

请问公园怎么走（qǐng wèn gōng yuán zěn me zǒu）？

Could you please tell me how to get to the park?

洗手间在什么地方（xǐ shǒu jiān zài shén me dì fāng）？

Can you show me the way to the toilet?

附近有饭店吗（fù jìn yǒu fàn diàn ma）？

Are there any restaurants nearby?

这趟车去不去机场（zhè tàng chē qù bú qù jī chǎng）？

Is this vehicle heading to the airport?

向前直走（xiàng qián zhí zǒu）。

Go straight.

向左拐（xiàng zuǒ guǎi）。

Turn left.

你得去马路对面坐车（nǐ děi qù mǎ lù duì miàn zuò chē）。

You have to get a taxi across the street.

这是什么地方（zhè shì shén me dì fāng）？

What is this place?

我们现在在哪里（wǒ men xiàn zài zài nǎ lǐ）？

Where are we?

走这边还是那边（zǒu zhè biān hái shì nà biān）？

Shall we go this way or that way?

去火车站到哪下（qù huǒ chē zhàn dào nǎ xià）？

Where should I get off the bus if I need to go to the train station?

Things Related to Time

现在几点了（xiàn zài jǐ diǎn le）？

What time is it now?

今天几号（jīn tiān jǐ hào）？

What day is today?

明天星期几（míng tiān xīng qī jǐ）？

What day is tomorrow?

你什么时候有空（nǐ shén me shí hòu yǒu kòng）？

When will you be free?

周末我没时间（zhōu mò wǒ méi shí jiān）。

I'm busy on the weekend.

你几点到几点上班（nǐ jǐ diǎn dào jǐ diǎn shàng bān）。

What time do you work?

我明天九点来找你（wǒ míng tiān jiǔ diǎn lái zhǎo nǐ）。

I'll come to get you tomorrow at 9 o'clock.

请晚上八点后打电话（qǐng wǎn shàng bā diǎn hòu dǎ diàn huà）。

Please call me after 8pm.

你等多久了（nǐ děng duō jiǔ le）？

How long you have been waiting?

我们在这学习一个月（wǒ men zài zhè xué xíyígè yuè）。

We will study here for a month.

火车几点开（huǒ chē jǐ diǎn kāi）？

When will the train leave?

飞机什么时候起飞（fēi jīshénme shí hòu qǐ fēi）？

When will the plane depart?

明天几点到北京（míng tiān jǐ diǎn dào běi jīng）？

When will you arrive in Beijing tomorrow?

你们哪天回家（nǐ men nǎ tiān huí jiā）？

What day are you going back home?

你打算什么时候再来（nǐ dǎ suàn shén me shí hòu zài lái）？

When are you planning to come back?

Business Negotiation

鉴于这几年的良好合作关系，我们准备接受你方的价格（jiàn yú zhè jǐ nián de liáng hǎo hé zuò guān xì, wǒ men zhǔn bèi jiē shòu nǐ fāng de jià gé）。

In view of our good cooperation over the past few years, we are prepared to accept your offer.

我认为我们应该各自折中一下以便业务成交（wǒ rèn wéi wǒ men yīng gāi gè zì zhé zhōng yíxià yǐ biàn yè wù chéng jiāo）。

I think we should come to a compromise with each other so as to close the deal.

若双方各自做些让步，生意是很容易达成的（ruò shuāng fāng gè zì zuò xiē ràng bù, shēng yì shì hěn róng yì dá chéng de）。

Business is quite possible if both sides make some concessions.

我们准备降低价格（wǒ men zhǔn bèi jiàng dī jià gé）。

We're ready to decrease the price.

百分之十的折扣太离谱了，我们准备给你百分之四（bǎi fèn zhī shí de zhékòu tài lí pǔ le, wǒ men zhǔn bèi gěi nǐ bǎi fèn zhī sì）。

A 10% discount is off the table, but we're willing to offer you 6%

Asking for Help

对不起，我要下车（duì bú qǐ, wǒ yào xià chē）。

Sorry, I need to get off (the vehicle).

你能帮我一个忙吗（nǐ néng bāng wǒ yí gè máng ma）?

Can you do me a favor?

麻烦你帮帮我吧（má fán nǐ bāng bang wǒ ba）。

Please help me.

你有什么事（nǐ yǒu shén me shì）？

What's up?

你怎么了（nǐ zěn me le）？

What happened?

请送我去医院（qǐng sòng wǒ qù yī yuàn）。

Please take me to the hospital.

快叫警察（kuài jiào jǐng chá）！

Call the police!

救命（jiù mìng）！

Help!

怎么办（zěn me bàn）？

What should I do?

我迷路了（wǒ mí lù le）。

I'm lost.

我的机票丢了（wǒ de jī piào diū le）。

I lost my plane ticket.

可以用一下你的手机吗（kě yǐ yòng yíxià nǐ de shǒu jī ma）？

Can I borrow your cellphone?

你真是太好了（nǐ zhēn shì tài hǎo le）！

That's so nice of you.

非常感谢（fēi cháng gǎn xiè）！

Thank you so much.

Saying Goodbye

时间过得真快（shí jiān guò dé zhēn kuài）。

Time flies.

我们来跟您告别（wǒ men lái gēn nín gào bié）。

We've come to say goodbye to you.

请收下这个小礼物（qǐng shōu xià zhè gè xiǎo lǐ wù）。

Please accept this small gift.

希望你喜欢（xī wàng nǐ xǐ huān）。

I hope you like it.

你给了我很多帮助（nǐ gěi le wǒ hěn duō bāng zhù）。

You've helped me a lot.

感谢你为我们做的一切（gǎn xiè nǐ wèi wǒ men zuò de yíqiē）。

Thank you for everything you've done for us.

希望以后还能再见面（xī wàng yǐ hòu hái néng zài jiàn miàn）。

I hope we can see each other again in the future.

能给我您的联系地址吗（néng gěi wǒ nín de lián xì dì zhǐ ma）？

Can you give me your contact address?

你有电子邮箱地址吗（nǐ yǒu diàn zǐ yóu xiāng dì zhǐ ma）？

Do you have an email address?

请一定要联系我（qǐng yídìng yào lián xì wǒ）。

Please contact me sometime.

我会想你的（wǒ huì xiǎng nǐ de）。

I'll miss you.

祝友谊地久天长（zhù yǒu yì dì jiǔ tiān zhǎng）。

Friendship lasts forever.

Conclusion

The above are some directions and suggestions about learning Chinese. You may use the book flexibly according to the actual situations. For total beginners, this is your entry-level Chinese learning material. We strive to make Chinese easier to learn so that our readers can study the language happily, effortlessly, and efficiently.

When laying stress on function, as well as listening and speaking drills, we have made every effort to observe the rules of language teaching by proceeding from the simple to the more complex and advancing in ordered steps. The examples are simple, practical, easy to lean and remember, and are representative of natural speech.

Here are some tips for you when you start or continue to learn to speak Chinese.

1. After you are familiar with the examples above, read them loudly and clearly. This is to use your listening ability to potentially strengthen your memory, and correct the pronunciation – you will find it much better than reading silently. That said, do make sure that you pronounce the sentences correctly.

2. Study frequently and form a habit. Spending a little time each day learning Chinese is better than learning it for quite a long time once a week. Always slice the study time into several short periods rather than in a continued long term. For example, you can use the time when taking the bus, having a meal, queuing in the line, or in the bath to learn new knowledge and continuously review.

3. Make vocabulary cards. Handmade vocabulary cards can help you improve the character recognition capabilities. In accordance with part of speech (verbs, nouns, etc.) to itemize them, carry around, and have them available to reference at any time.

4. Bedtime review. Some people found that a quick five-minute review before going to sleep can enhance memory. This review should not be time-consuming and not suitable at midnight, because while your body is still awake, your brain is already trying to sleep.

5. Find yourself a practice partner. Find a Chinese pal and talk with him/her; you will not only learn how to speak Chinese correctly but also acquire a lot more knowledge about Chinese culture and life experience. They can strengthen their English in the meantime--two birds killed with one stone.

6. Once you are familiar with Chinese characters, you can block the Pinyin part – what you're doing is trying to understand the meaning of the sentences, not the pronunciation. Developing this habit will make your future learning easier.

7. Enroll in some language course so you can learn Chinese with experienced teachers who can help you precisely locate your current Chinese level and rapidly improve it via professional techniques.

Finally, just remember; don't be too harsh on yourself! Learning a language is a gradual process--you have to keep at it. To be honest, Chinese is one of the hardest languages to learn, so take your time. Once you feel comfortable with the basics of Chinese speech, consider taking a trip to China. Nothing can be better for learning the language than a journey to its native land!

CPSIA information can be obtained
at www.ICGtesting.com
Printed in the USA
LVHW010906100722
723072LV00004B/187